Islam and War

Islam and War

A Study in Comparative Ethics

JOHN KELSAY

Westminster/John Knox Press
Louisville, Kentucky

Book design by Laura Lee

First edition

Published by Westminster/John Knox Press
Louisville, Kentucky

This book is printed on acid-free paper that meets the American National Standards Institute Z39.48 standard.

PRINTED IN THE UNITED STATES OF AMERICA
9 8 7 6 5 4 3 2 1

Library of Congress Cataloging-in-Publication Data

Kelsay, John
   Islam and war : a study in comparative ethics / John Kelsay.—1st ed.
      p.   cm.
   Includes index.
   ISBN 0-664-25302-4 (alk. paper)

   1. War—Religious aspects—Islam. 2. Just war doctrine.
3. Persian Gulf War, 1991—Religious aspects. 4. Hussein, Saddam, 1937–   —Views on Islam and war. 5. War—Moral and ethical aspects. I. Title.
BP190.5.W35K44 1993
297'.5—dc20   92-33117

Contents

Acknowledgments

In this book, citations from the Qurʾan are drawn, with the author's revisions, from the translation by Mohammed Marmaduke Pickthall, *The Meaning of the Glorious Koran* (London: Unwin-Hyman, 1976).

Portions of chapters 1 and 6 appeared in another form in John Kelsay, "Are Wars of Religion Returning? Thoughts on the Legacy of Saddam Hussein," *In Depth* 2, no.1 (Winter 1992): 97–114. Used by permission.

Portions of chapters 3 and 4 are taken from John Kelsay, "Islam and the Distinction Between Combatants and Noncombatants," in James Turner Johnson and John Kelsay, eds., *Cross, Crescent, and Sword: Justification and Limitation of War in Western and Islamic Tradition* (Westport, Conn.: Greenwood Press, 1990), pp. 197–220. Portions of chapter 4 also appeared in John Kelsay, "Religion, Morality, and the Governance of War: The Case of Classical Islam," *Journal of Religious Ethics* 18, no. 2 (Fall 1990): 123–139. Used by permission of Religious Ethics, Inc.

Material from *Charter of the Islamic Resistance Movement (Hamas) of Palestine*, trans. Muhammad Maqdsi (Dallas: Islamic Association for Palestine, 1990), is used by permission. Please note: The views expressed in that publication are not those of the Islamic Association for Palestine.

Material from Majid Khadduri, *The Islamic Law of Nations: Shaybani's Siyar* (Baltimore: Johns Hopkins University Press, 1966) is used by permission.

Material from Johannes J. G. Jansen, *The Neglected Duty* (New York: Macmillan, 1986) is used by permission.

Author's Note on Arabic Terms

In writing this book, I have tried to minimize the use of Arabic terminology. Some terms are unavoidable, however. In those cases, I have generally followed the system of transliteration recommended by the Library of Congress. I have also, however, made use of current English-language conventions for some terms. The most important examples are the use of *Shiite* in place of *Shiʿi* and of *Baathist* in place of *Baʾthist* or *Baʾathist*.

Introduction

Over the last thirty years, perhaps no issue in religious ethics has attracted more consistent attention than the use of force in war. Inspired by the attempts of Fr. John Courtney Murray and Paul Ramsey to recover the just war tradition for theological ethics, more recent writers have been interested in philosophical and historical inquiries concerning the ethics of war: in analyses of the "moral logic" of the just war criteria or of the "sources" of the just war tradition in Western culture, for example. Joined with all such inquiries are the practical questions that engage not only students of ethics but morally concerned persons everywhere: How does one measure the justice of war—in general, and also in particular cases? What are the rules of war? Who has authority to declare war, and when? By what criteria do we evaluate modern weapons, especially weapons capable of mass destruction? The public attention commanded in recent years by the issues connected with nuclear deterrence, the debate over strategic defense initiatives, and the intense (and, as of June 1992, ongoing) discussion over the question of war in the Persian Gulf illustrate the extent to which attention to questions of the ethics of force has become a part of the moral landscape of European and North American culture.

The Persian Gulf War, however, called to attention an important gap in almost all the contemporary literature on ethics and war: the lack of attention to cross-cultural or comparative perspectives. Recent debates in Europe and North America have concerned the nature, sources, and application of Western traditions on the morality of war. The work of James Turner Johnson, for example, has consistently called attention to the ways that diverse sources of just war tradition

1

can and do inform contemporary moral debate: Hebrew Scriptures, Roman law, Germanic codes for knights, canon law, Christian theology, and international law all have their place in providing Western culture with a vocabulary to discuss the relations between ethics and war.[1] But there is no comparable body of work on non-European, non-North American traditions.[2] Some of the questions raised during the Gulf War cry out for the kind of information that would be provided by such work: By what standards (if any) was Iraq's annexation of Kuwait justified? What was the morality of Iraqi missile attacks on civilian populations in Tel Aviv, Riyadh, Dhahran, and other cities during January and February of 1991? And, since President Saddam Hussein made extensive use of Islamic terminology in public statements before, during, and after the war in the Gulf, what is the teaching of Islam on questions of the use of force in war? Is there an Islamic "just war tradition" or not?

This book attempts to address the current lack of comparative perspectives on the ethics of war, particularly with respect to Islam. In one sense, the volume is a response to discussions occasioned by the Gulf War, with particular attention to the role of Islam in Iraqi policy. Indeed, a number of the chapters printed here were originally given as talks delivered to groups interested in understanding the confrontation of the Allied forces with Iraq. My own position, however, is that citizens, policymakers, and students of religious ethics need to push beyond this most recent crisis in an attempt to gain broader, more historically oriented perspectives on the role of Islam in statecraft, particularly with respect to war. Whatever Saddam Hussein's flaws, he understood that the confrontation in the Persian Gulf is but one part of a complex network of relationships between the two cultural traditions we currently describe as "Western" and "Islamic." Through an analysis of Islamic perspectives on ethics and the use of force, I propose to lay plain some portions of that network, in the interests of promoting deeper understanding of the relationships that prevail between ethics, war, and the practice of politics across cultural lines.

The "method" here employed involves the creation of a kind of comparative dialogue in the mind of the reader. Notions that are familiar (issues connected with the just war tradition) serve as benchmarks in the attempt to understand classical and contemporary Islamic notions on the justification and conduct of war.[3] Thus, for example, the struggle of just war thinkers with the question, "Can religion ever serve as a just cause of war?" forms the background for introducing a distinctive emphasis of Islamic thought: that is, that the only "just" war is one fought for religious purposes. I expect persons schooled in the just war tradition to find this position troublesome. I also hope that, in coming to grips with the arguments of Muslims, such persons will appreciate the lively and powerful critique of all forms of "secularism" that drives this aspect of Islamic thought. The "internal dialogue" resulting from such an approach can, it seems to me, serve any or all of the following audiences and purposes: scholars of religious ethics and their students interested in deepening their reflections upon the possible connections between ethics and war; policymakers considering the role of Islam in world politics, and concerned to honor the principle "Know your adversary"; moralists wishing to respond to James Turner Johnson's suggestion[4] that the current task facing advocates of the just war tradition of limiting war is to turn the theoretical universality of that tradition into a practical universality, particularly by incorporating non-European and non-North American religious and moral perspectives into the tradition; and ordinary citizens concerned about the conflict between the West and Islam. My hope in writing has been to produce a volume accessible to, and therefore useful for, all these audiences.

In outline, the argument proceeds as follows.

Chapter 1 begins with the war in the Gulf, focusing especially on the role of Islamic symbols in the rhetoric of Iraqi president Saddam Hussein. As I try to indicate, the superficiality (or, as many put it, hypocrisy) of the Iraqi president's use of Islamic terminology matters less than one might think. In particular, the context in which President Hussein spoke is one in which there exists a great variety of opinion concerning the proper relation of historic Islamic symbols to contemporary political problems. The Allied nations won the war. But Saddam Hussein continues in power—for some, that provides reason enough to say that the desperate hopes for justice to which the Iraqi president spoke during the crisis remain alive and continue to play an important role in understanding certain aspects of the place of Islam in world politics. In the long run, I argue that we must get beyond the Gulf War and Saddam Hussein, however: Islam's diverse and powerful witness to the responsibility of humanity before and under God reaches much farther than Saddam Hussein was able to show. To put it another way, understanding the political potential of Islam requires a more detailed reading of that tradition's sources than a focus on the Iraqi president is likely to yield. To facilitate that process, I provide some basic information about the Islamic tradition. Some readers may wish to skip the latter pages of this chapter and go on to the next. My feeling is that some will desire such information, however, and that it is therefore worth including.

Chapter 2 provides an overview of the Islamic tradition on these relations. In Islam, as in the Western tradition, discussions of war do not occur in isolation from the more general discussion of ethical and political responsibilities. When Augustine of Hippo (d. 430) wrote that the goal of war is peace he stated a truth that runs counter to much of modern thinking about war. Yet Augustine's maxim is profoundly a part of those religious and moral traditions which try to connect ethics, war, and statecraft. That being the case, our focus in beginning to understand the Islamic tradition should be on its view of the nature and requirements of peace. The Muslim understanding of the connections between ethics, war, and political action becomes clearer as a result.

Chapter 2 ends with a set of comparative observations that provide the rationale for three subsequent essays on "points for discussion" between the Western and Islamic traditions on ethics and war. Each of these essays follows a similar pattern: identification of an issue between the two traditions; discussion of classical Islamic perspectives, followed by contemporary examples. There is considerable overlap in the Islamic materials discussed in each essay; my hope is that this will provide continuity to the discussion as readers engage rather disparate issues. Chapter 3, then, focuses on the notion of religion as a just cause of war. As I have already indicated, students of the just war tradition, schooled in Victoria's notion that difference in religion can never be a just cause of war, will probably find strange the Islamic contention that religion is in fact *the only* just cause for military action. And yet, I believe that just war thinkers will find that Islamic reasoning on this point has considerable connection with historic experience and involves a powerful argument about the best ways to restrain that will-to-power which so often shows itself in the human ability to justify force, even in excess, in the pursuit of personal or communal gain.

Chapter 4 takes up the question, so important to contemporary just war thinking, of the basis and scope of noncombatant immunity. I argue that Islamic tradition shares with the just war tradition a concern to discriminate between the innocent and the guilty—to ensure that the latter are punished in war, while the former are not. Yet the Islamic perspective on innocence and guilt, and its rationale for identifying certain persons as noncombatants, is quite different from the version of immunity common to contemporary just war thought. Again, I expect just war thinkers to experience this discrepancy between the two traditions as disconcerting, at first glance. But the dialogue can serve to remind students of just war tradition of certain gaps in their own understanding of the ways that the prohibition of murder should be applied in the context of war.

Chapter 5 takes up the vexed question of "irregular" wars: wars in which one or more forces fight without the official sanction of an established political entity. The classical Islamic tradition presents a perspective on rebellion, in particular, that just war thinking did not approximate until the nineteenth century. At the same time, the questions of how an irregular force (1) can have authority to engage in military action and (2) avoids the tendency to engage in indiscriminate violence are perhaps the most important points of contention in the contemporary Islamic discussion of ethics and war.

The subject of irregular war, in particular, moves the discussion back to current events, even to the rhetoric of Saddam Hussein. There can be no doubt that President Hussein's intention, at least, was to engage some of the same sense of injustice that gives rise to contemporary militant groups. Thus chapter 6 attempts to set the material from the preceding chapters in context. The vehicle is the discussion of the New World Order. As I write, George Bush's use of this notion in connection with the war in the Gulf is already largely forgotten. But the notion is a useful way of raising important questions for students of ethics and for concerned people in general. What, for example, shall we say about the relationship of the West and Islam? What are the possibilities for moral and political cooperation between cultures whose people speak in terms of similar symbols, yet often find themselves far apart on issues of policy? Overall, my conclusion is rather pessimistic: the New World Order is more rhetoric than reality. One cannot deny certain persistent commonalities between the Western and Islamic traditions on ethics, war, and politics, however. Both speak to the effect that war must serve legitimate aims; both are concerned to limit the resort to and damage of war. Both worry about problems posed by the human capacity for self-interest and self-deception; in this regard, both try to motivate the moral conscience of humanity as a means of discriminating between just and unjust action. Perhaps such commonalities serve, in the main, to indicate the nature of disagreement between the West and Islam. Given the differing accounts of modern history that prevail in the two cultures, there is a certain inevitability in that fact. But there should be no doubt that, in certain contexts, the common discourse about ethics and war shared by these two traditions has the potential for creative and cooperative endeavor. Given the increased presence of Muslims in Europe and North America—a presence that makes for a more intense interaction between the two traditions than ever before—it is important to see this. Thus I close with an account of an exchange that occurred at a spring 1992 conference in Washington, D.C., on the question, How should Muslims (particularly in North America) view the relationship of the Gulf War to the Islamic tradition on ethics, war, and statecraft? I think the exchange was healthy and has promise for the self-understanding of all those identified with "the West" and/or "Islam."

In writing this book, I have been encouraged by a number of people, only some of whom I can mention. James F. Childress, Kyle Professor of Ethics at the University of Virginia, was my first teacher in matters of the just war tradition. To him, as to Abdulaziz Sachedina and David Little, I owe the kind of debts that every student owes—debts that really can never be repaid. In 1987, just at the beginning of my career, Jim Johnson was willing to join me in submitting a grant to the United States Institute of Peace for a series of conferences on Western and Islamic approaches to war and peace. While Jim has never pressed the point, I feel certain that the Institute's willingness to fund the conferences rested, by and large, on the association of his name with the proposal. It certainly could not have rested on mine, which was (still is!) largely known only to my family and a few friends. The papers from those conferences, published in two volumes by Greenwood Press, added a great deal to my understanding of the issues discussed in this book. I certainly want to thank the scholars who contributed them and whose observations continue to interest and instruct me.[5]

In the fall of 1987 I began teaching in the Department of Religion at Florida State University. From the first day, my colleagues have expressed interest in and support for my work; I am grateful especially for the encouragement offered with respect to this book by Richard L. Rubenstein, the Robert O. Lawton Distinguished Professor of Religion at FSU. Outside my own department, Jeff Tatum, Associate Professor of Classics, has been a good friend and has read more of my work than anyone should have to.

Finally, I want to express thanks to Rita and to our children: David, Marybekah, and Elizabeth. They love me, whether or not I write books like this. Yet I hope that one day they can feel that, with this and other projects, their husband and father made a contribution they can be proud of. This book is dedicated to them.

CHAPTER ONE

The Gulf War and Beyond: Thoughts on the Legacy of Saddam Hussein

The late Protestant theologian Reinhold Niebuhr used to say there were two ways in which human beings work out the anxiety basic to their existence—hubris, or overweening pride, and apatheia. Whatever our opinions of Iraqi president Saddam Hussein, we surely cannot accuse him of apathy. From the time he burst onto the Arab scene in the 1960s to his current struggle to maintain power in postwar Iraq, Saddam Hussein has played his cards for all they are worth. As some have put it, he has raised the art of political brinksmanship to new heights.

If President Hussein's political career can be said to demonstrate any principle, it would be (as *New York Times* analyst Thomas Friedman once pointed out) the one expressed in the Arab proverb *"haraka, baraka"* ("movement is a blessing"). For motion, activity has, more than success, kept Saddam Hussein alive politically—that, and the willingness to use force to keep the lid on the have-nots among Iraq's highly diverse population.

We are now at some distance from the Gulf War. Iraq's armies have been defeated, its people wracked not only by Allied bombing during the war (immediately after the war a U.N. Commission described Iraq as reduced to a preindustrial state) but by bloody fighting in which Saddam Hussein's forces attempted to repress rebellions by Kurds and Shiites. To this date (June 1992), President Hussein has outlasted every attempt to oust him. His power is reduced, yet he remains a force in Middle Eastern politics.

What will become of Saddam Hussein? My own guess is that he will remain in power for some time. Let us suppose, however, that I am wrong—that death or rebellion may remove Iraq's president from the political scene. We shall still have to deal with a certain inheritance—what I am calling "the legacy of Saddam Hussein." The ideas that President Hussein articulated in speeches during the Gulf Crisis and subsequent war will live on—not because he is a particularly creative thinker, or even a specially exemplary leader, but because Iraq's confrontation with the West provided him with an opportunity to express judgments and aspirations common to a significant number of Arabs, Muslims, and others. To summarize, and thus oversimplify these: There is a double standard in world politics. For the West and its friends, the present international order provides freedom, security, dignity. But for Arabs, Muslims, and developing nations, there is only oppression, exploitation, and dishonor. It is time the oppressed stood up for their rights, with the Muslims bearing the standard for justice and equity against an irreligious, morally bankrupt West.

It is my premise that many Western scholars and policymakers have underestimated—or perhaps "mis-estimated"—the importance of Saddam Hussein's speeches as a way of understanding world politics. That they have done so is largely due to an inadequate appreciation of the power of the religious symbols he used in the events following the August 1990 invasion of Kuwait. When the Iraqi president characterized his struggle with the Allied forces as a jihad, for example, most observers dismissed this as a crude, political use of the term. How could a man who has consistently presented himself as a "secular" Arab leader expect to be taken seriously when he resorted to the traditional language of Islam?

Crude and political uses of symbols can have great significance, however. If we do not take President Hussein seriously and try to understand how his call for jihad fits in the religious and political culture of the Middle East, then we shall be less likely to develop the kinds of policy initiatives necessary to deal with challenges that are coming in the next decade. Saddam Hussein is, in one sense, only the most visible manifestation of trends within Arab and Islamic culture that we shall have to deal with in the years ahead. To develop understanding that will serve us well, we must go beyond the Gulf War and begin to deal with the history of Islamic thought on ethics, war, and politics. As a first step, I propose that we glance back at the war in the Gulf and analyze the rhetoric of Saddam Hussein.

Saddam Hussein and His Challenge

The Gulf War inflicted sorrow and suffering on many people. One may be forgiven, however, for mentioning the one group for which it was a veritable bonanza: political analysts. Of the many words produced for newspapers and magazines, or on television or radio, none has yet proven more suggestive than that spoken by an Arab journalist on the MacNeil-Lehrer program just a few weeks after the invasion of Kuwait. What, he was asked, is foremost on your mind as Iraqi forces solidify their occupation of Kuwait, Allied troops move into the area, and war seems a strong possibility?

Hearkening back to the presidential campaign of 1988, the journalist said words to this effect: "I wish I could speak to Saddam Hussein. And if I could, I would be very blunt with him. I would borrow a phrase from Senator Lloyd Bentsen, from his debate with Vice President Quayle. And I would say: Mr. President, I have known Gamal Abd al-Nasser. I have been with Gamal Abd al-Nasser and seen him work. Mr. Saddam Hussein, you are no Gamal Abd al-Nasser."

One laughs at this borrowed put-down. But no one should miss the symbolic reference in this journalist's remark. Gamal Abd al-Nasser is the key to deciphering important portions of Saddam Hussein's rhetoric in the weeks that led up to the war in the Gulf. Following the invasion of Kuwait, when the Iraqi president found himself faced with an international boycott and large numbers of European and American troops in Saudi Arabia, he called for a jihad, a "holy war." But he did so in a very particular way, in which the strictly Islamic dimensions of jihad were mingled with notions of Arab nationalism and the struggle of developing nations for economic and political justice. On August 10, for example, President Hussein spoke to "all Arab and Muslim masses wherever they are," calling on them to "save Mecca and the Tomb of the Prophet [in Medina] from occupation." As he then put it:

> The Arab state of affairs has changed after the foreigner entered their lands and Western colonialism divided and established weak states ruled by families that offered him services that facilitated their mission. The colonialists, to insure their petroleum interests, . . . set up those disfigured petroleum states. Through this, they kept the wealth away from the masses of this nation [i.e., the Arab nation]. This new wealth came into the hands of the few to be exploited for the benefit of the foreigner and those few new rulers. . . . Financial and social corruption spread. The imperialists, deviators, merchants, political agents, the servants of the foreigner and Zionism all stood up against Iraq only because it represents the conscience of the Arab nation and its ability to safeguard its honor and rights against any harm. Iraq, O Arabs, is your Iraq. . . . It is the candle of right to snuff out darkness.

Iraq, the president concluded, is "determined to carry out jihad without any hesitation or retreat and without any fear from the foreigner's power."[1]

Now, it was significant, as the *New York Times* told its readers, that Saddam Hussein, who was usually considered a "secular" leader, had called for a jihad. And there was some truth to the subsequent observation of President George Bush, to the effect that this was the rhetoric of a desperate man. But it is also finally true that Saddam Hussein's rhetoric was intended for a particular audience and that the Iraqi president spoke out of a particular legacy. Overall, the themes in this and other speeches echoed those articulated in Gamal Abd al-Nasser's "philosophy of revolution," a set of ideas that fired the imagination of an entire generation of Arab leaders during the 1950s and 1960s. Nasser foresaw a world revolution in three interlocking circles: first and foremost, the revolution of the Arabs, in which a people with a common language and history would throw off the yoke of colonialism. This first circle would, however, find increased strength and secure its aims only as it joined with the revolution of Muslims unified by faith; and also with that of developing nations, responding to those who would exploit their abundant natural resources. Saddam Hussein was one of those inspired by Nasser's ideals. It was Nasser, after all, who sponsored the young Iraqi's early progress in Arab nationalist circles. The rhetoric of Arab unity had always been a part of Saddam Hussein's public platform. In one sense, then, it was not strange that the Iraqi leader's call for jihad should resonate with the great Egyptian's political philosophy. The struggle of Arabs against the colonial powers of Europe and North America; the idea of Muslims defending the holy sites of Islam against foreigners and non-Muslims; the depiction of Iraq's confrontation with the Allied forces as part of the struggle for social justice—all of this was stock-in-trade for Nasser and for his disciple.

In another sense, however, Saddam Hussein's use of this rhetoric was strange. According to most observers, "Nasserism" died with its charismatic leader in 1970. One could almost say that the "philosophy of revolution" ceased to be viable following Nasser's defeat at the hands of Israel in the June 1967 war. Indeed, by 1981 no less an observer than Fouad Ajami could speak of the emptiness of Arab nationalism.[2] Not that people renounced Nasser. On the contrary, he was revered. But the solidarity of which Nasser had spoken came to rest in the no-man's-land of political ideology. It became the kind of idea that every Arab gave lip service to but that no one was willing to sacrifice for. Even during the long war between Iraq and Iran, when Arab nations lined up to support their "brothers' struggle," Arab cooperation owed more to the fear of revolutionary Islam than to any real sense of unity. Finally, there is a sense in which Iraq's invasion of Kuwait signified the absolute nadir of Nasser's pan-Arab ideals. How else was one to interpret the "rape of Kuwait," except as an admission that the various Arab states had little in the way of common interests that might enable them to settle problems without the use of force? By most accounts, the ideals of Nasserism were far removed from the minds of Iraq's ruling elite when the decision was taken to invade Kuwait. What came first was cash, and closely connected with that, oil. Iraq's internal problems were very great, not least in connection with the famous "one million man" army built during the war with Iran. How, after all, does a nation deal with idle young men after they have learned the demeanor and power that come from bearing weapons and wearing uniforms?

One should not argue that ideals were a part of Iraq's invasion mentality. Even the dusting off of an old and dubious argument about Kuwait as the nineteenth province of Iraq was only made post-invasion, when the world community expressed opposition to Iraq.

The post-invasion context, however, is the key to Saddam Hussein's decision to employ the rhetoric of his mentor. Once Iraq encountered international opposition, President Hussein found himself in a new context, higher in risks and in potential benefits. If he could somehow "ennoble" his action; rekindle some aspects of Nasser's philosophy, or wrap himself in the mantle of Islam and social justice—then he might come out of this crisis not only with economic and military power but with new prestige. He would then have resolved what Max Weber called the problem of legitimation—a problem that almost every leader in the Middle East shares.[3]

Once President Hussein invoked Nasser's version of jihad, the great question became, "Can he succeed?" At the most obvious level, the answer proved negative. The crisis in the Gulf led to a devastating war, in which much of Iraq's military capacity was destroyed. The Baathist regime in Baghdad was forced to deal with a degree of unrest among the Kurdish and Shiite minorities unparalleled in the modern history of Iraq. Indeed, the problems of the Kurds may yet end in a partition of the nation. Suffering among civilians has evidently been very great. And it will be impossible to estimate for several years the impact on Iraq's future of the deaths of the many young men conscripted into service who died during Allied bombing raids.

At the same time, President Hussein and his advisers apparently believe there is a sense in which Iraq can claim victory. Following the war, Iraqi officials immediately began to speak of their hope for a day when Arabs and Muslims would see that Iraq had acted with courage on behalf of oppressed peoples everywhere. Within a few weeks after the war, just after his armies finished with the Shiites in southern Iraq, Saddam Hussein began to make public appearances around the country. Standing on a platform, speaking to the people, the president of Iraq would brandish a pistol, firing shots into the air, while people chanted his greatness. The message: Iraq was damaged, but Saddam was bigger than Iraq. He was here to stay.

It is difficult to imagine, following reports of the suffering in Iraq; but as of autumn 1991 there was even evidence to suggest that some people outside Iraq believed President Hussein's claims of success. Reports from Jordan, the West Bank, and Gaza indicated that numerous Palestinians representing a wide spectrum of economic and educational backgrounds subscribed to something like the following judgment: Saddam Hussein is an Arab hero. He may have made some mistakes, but he stood up to the imperialists. He did something, while others stood passively by. He kept his word: Saddam said he would bomb Tel Aviv, and he did. He said he would develop weapons the equal of Israel's, and he was well on the way, before the United Nations, led by imperialist powers like the United States, forced him to choose between turning over nuclear information and the further devastation of his people. Who knows? Even now, Iraq may be developing such weapons. So long as Saddam survives, hope lives on.

One can ask questions that are troubling, even to those who hold such opinions. But again, answers could be found. What about the destruction of Iraq? Answer: Obviously not as bad as the Western media portrayed, since Saddam is still in power and his armies were strong enough to put down the Kurds and the Shiites. What about criticisms voiced by Iraqis—dissidents, both inside and outside the country—to the effect that the Baathist regime has brought suffering to the people of Iraq? Answer: The Iraqi people suffered at the hands of Western powers. They were victims of injustice. President Hussein and his supporters are working as quickly as possible to restore Iraq to normal. Their critics should know that, by supporting foreigners who want to bring the government down, they will prolong the suffering of the Iraqi people. And so on.

As Saddam Hussein's troubles have continued, such support seems to have faltered a bit. The opinions serve, however, to illustrate this point: the war in the Gulf was *not* "just about oil."[4] Nor was it only a matter of numbers of troops and military capacity. Saddam Hussein knew the context in which he spoke. Once he began to employ the rhetoric of his mentor, Gamal Abd al-Nasser; once he spoke of Iraq's confrontation with the coalition forces as a jihad, the Gulf

War came to involve prestige, moral authority—even religion. Those who characterized this rhetorical style as hypocritical or crude were, in one sense, missing the point. Saddam Hussein did not have to be religious, or even a particularly moral man, to make effective use of symbols that suggest the highest ideals and motivations of people in the Middle East. Nor did he have to meet all the requirements of Islamic religious law to rally people to his banner. What he had to do—and in my judgment, did with some degree of success—was to relate these symbols to his own cause. For Saddam Hussein, the one uncertainty was the response of the coalition. He gambled that the United States and its Allies would not fight to the finish. He lost—at least, in the short run. From his point of view, the battle is not over yet.

To return to our experiment: Suppose Saddam Hussein is removed from the political scene, by whatever means. What exactly is his legacy? What does he represent, such that the world would need to deal with his ideas, even should the man be taken from power?

The answer, for many of those who admired the Iraqi president's stand in the Gulf, lies in his appeal to Islam. I have already said that President Hussein's mix of appeals to Arabs, Muslims, and the developing nations was a restatement of the philosophy of his mentor, Gamal Abd al-Nasser. But that is not the whole story. Times change, and so does political rhetoric. While Saddam Hussein spoke as a disciple of Nasser, he also spoke in the wake of the Iranian revolution; of eight long years of war between Iraq and Iran; and of the general revival of religious discourse that has characterized much of the Middle East since the early 1970s. Saddam's jihad was not strictly Islamic. But it was put in terms more clearly religious than Nasser would have employed. Thus, on September 5, 1990, the Iraqi president declared that the crisis in the Gulf

is the great crisis of this age in this part of the world where the material side of life has surpassed the spiritual one and the moral one. . . . This is the war of right against wrong and is a crisis between Allah's teachings and the devil. Allah the Almighty has made his choice—the choice for the fighters and the strugglers who are in favor of principles. God has chosen the arena for this crisis to be the Arab World, and has put the Arabs in a progressive position in which the Iraqis are among the foremost. And to confirm once more the meaning that God taught us ever since the first light of faith and belief, which is that the arena of the Arab world is the arena of the first belief and Arabs have always been an example and a model for belief and faith in God Almighty and are the ones who are worthy of true happiness. It is now your turn,

Arabs, to save all humanity and not just save yourselves, and to show the principles and meanings of the message of Islam, of which you are all believers and of which you are all leaders.[5]

More than most, Saddam Hussein sought to blend the rhetoric of Arab history and pride with the Islamic sense of mission. The world, he argued, is a testing ground. God created it in order to see which of God's creatures will outdo the others in doing good. Thus humanity has its destiny: to command good and forbid evil, and to establish a just social order. Within that general destiny, the Arab nation has a special place, for it was to that nation that Islam first came. Thus Saddam concludes: Now is the time to show what you are made of! Now is the time to bear witness to Islam!

Again, there were many to say that President Hussein's speech-making was all rhetoric and no substance. Where was his authority to declare a jihad? Where were his credentials as an Islamic scholar? Such questions are important. Again, however, they miss the point. For the people listening to Saddam Hussein, the words attributed to an unidentified Iraqi official were apt: If petrol is important to the Americans, Jerusalem is important to us. For Saddam Hussein, appeals to Islam may have been propaganda. The terms were crafted for his audience; the issue was prestige in the Arab community. But for many who heard him speak, the issue was justice and, connected with that, territory. In particular, the issue was, and is, the rightful hegemony of Islam in certain lands, including, though not exhausted by, the West Bank and Gaza.

The strength of President Hussein's appeal to Islam lay, not in his own piety or scholarship, but in the power of symbolic references: Saddam affirmed the greatness of the Arab people, as those given the first witness of Islam; he reminded Muslims of their vocation to illustrate the principles according to which human beings should live; he spoke of the necessity of struggle against evil and injustice throughout the earth; he identified certain places with the heritage of Islam. All of these are powerful themes in the history of Islam. President Hussein played them all, with some degree of success.

In Amman, Jordan, for example, the following exchange was reported between Crown Prince Hassan and the dean of the religious faculty at Amman University approximately a month before the war began. The prince is describing King Hussein's policy of seeking an "Arab solution" to the Gulf Crisis. It is, he says, the only way to avoid a "disastrous war." But the dean, who is from Nablus on the West Bank (and thus a Palestinian), stands and responds: "We need to prepare all the people for a jihad and turn Jordan into one big battlefield. . . . A great man once said, 'Now is the time to die.' And now is the best time to die."[6] Saddam put it somewhat differently: Now is the time to stand up for what is right, to bear witness for the faith. But the impulse was the same. To stand for justice, to participate in the Islamic mission, is to assert Palestinian and Islamic hegemony over land lost to imperialism. Those who stand in this way may die. But they will do so as martyrs in the path of God.

Still, this does not fully resolve the question of the legacy of Saddam Hussein. To understand that, we must turn again to post-war opinion. Again, Palestinians in Jordan, the West Bank, and Gaza are of interest. For there, it seems, one found an interesting Islamic approach to the question, "Who is Saddam Hussein, and what did he accomplish?" In brief, the answer was: Saddam is a leader who has done a service for the Muslim community.

Obviously, one can probe more deeply than this. What type of service did Saddam Hussein perform? At various times during the conflict, the Iraqi president recalled the example of Saladin, the great leader who drove the Crusaders out of Islamic territory. The implied conclusion was that Saddam Hussein would be a modern-day Saladin. If the Muslims would unite around him, the Europeans and the Americans could be driven out of the Arabian peninsula and a new era of justice be born.

As late as autumn of 1991, many Palestinians responded to this question as follows: We do not yet know the outcome of Saddam Hussein's struggle. He may be like Saladin; he may not. Regardless of the outcome, however, he has done a service. God used him to show the way for Palestinians, and indeed all the Muslims, to carry on their struggle. That way is through a return to Islam.

It is hardly news to say that the 1970s and 1980s have seen a revival of interest in Islamic piety in the Middle East. It is of interest, however, to note the pace of the revival among Palestinians following the Gulf War. The trend toward women adopting Islamic dress, the recurrence to Islam in ordinary discourse, and the visibility of organizations like the Muslim Brethren have not slowed after the Gulf War. If anything, in countries like Jordan, the revival has increased. And in the mosques, the message put before people is this: Saddam Hussein did not do wrong in appealing to Islam during the Gulf War. The problem was that he did not go far enough, particularly in the matter of adherence to Islamic law. Thus the faithful are asked to consider: What was Saddam Hussein's greatest virtue in the Gulf War? The answer: He appealed to Islam. Again: Why, then, did the Iraqi forces suffer defeat? Answer: Despite his turn to Islam, Saddam Hussein was not an entirely pure figure. He and his armies violated Islamic law by killing Muslims in Kuwait. So: What should the Muslim community learn from this? Answer: Saddam moved in the right direction. But he did not go far enough. Believers must now carry through—not necessarily in terms of military activity, but in a revival of piety and adherence to religious law. According to the Qur'an, God "never changes the condition of a people until they change themselves" (13:11). The path to victory begins with acceptance of the guidance that God has given. Acts of personal repentance and discipline build a people into a strong community. One cannot know precisely what the Muslim community will have to do to serve the cause of God in the coming years. One can only know that, if the Muslims are strong in the practice of their religion, they will be ready. The true power of Saddam Hussein's legacy, then, lies in the way he publicly articulated a religious interpretation of the confrontation between Iraq and the coalition forces. This, he said, "is the war of right against wrong and is a crisis between Allah's teachings and the devil." It was to be a crucial moment in the long struggle of Muslims to bear witness to the one God and to remind humanity of its responsibilities before God.

Islam and Its Mission

The Islamic tradition is broader and deeper than Saddam Hussein's speeches, of course. Already implied, even in the description of support for the Iraqi president's resistance to the coalition forces, is a judgment that his rhetoric did not go far enough. The appeal to Islam, while a step in the right direction, did not involve an affirmation of Islamic law. God requires obedience. True piety is shown by adherence to Islamic precepts. Thus the challenge Saddam Hussein posed to the Western powers needs to be strengthened by a deep renewal of Islamic faith.

For many Westerners, such talk is frightening. In recent years, Europeans and North Americans have come to associate Islam with a number of particularly unpleasant types of political behavior: hostage taking, suicide bombings, the announcement of a death sentence for author Salman Rushdie. The list goes on. As one writer puts it, "Muslim sensibilities do not register, except negatively, among Euro-American opinion setters."[7] What would a deep renewal of Islamic faith mean, except more unpleasantness?

For Muslims, by comparison, the issues raised by a call to faith are different. For some, the war in the Gulf helped to make the point that the West is implacably hostile to any attempt by Arabs and Muslims at self-assertion. The fact that the coalition forces included troops from Egypt, Saudi Arabia, and Syria does not alter the perception of Western antipathy. The leaders of those nations are incurably dependent on

Western power—economically, militarily, and politically. For such Muslims, Saddam Hussein's challenge led to a healthy, though painful, lesson in reality. The West will never willingly allow Muslims to determine their own destiny. The call to faith is necessary, as a summons to struggle for justice.

For others, the Gulf War was the latest in a series of tragic indicators of the depths to which Arabs and Muslims have been brought by two centuries of unbridled Western dominance. Europeans and Americans are not the only ones with a list of unpleasant political incidents. Many Muslims think of the destruction of Iraq in connection with the massacre of Palestinians at Sabra and Shatila, the Israeli invasion and occupation of southern Lebanon, and the general degradation of Islam in the Western media, most obviously in the publication of Salman Rushdie's *Satanic Verses*. For these Muslims, the call to Islamic renewal carries a certain danger, illustrated not least by the outcome of the Gulf War. One should be ready to die for one's faith, after all; but should one court death? To some, it seems that is what Saddam Hussein encouraged. The call to faith should thus include a counsel of prudence. But overall, it is healthy for Muslims to encourage renewal. Islam, after all, signifies a source of values that are the wellspring of a great civilization. It may even be that Muslims, by asserting themselves, will make the West more sensitive to the values it professes but does not live by.

One could continue to delineate shades of Muslim opinion. At bottom, however, all those seeking renewal are calling for a return to ways of thinking and acting that are based on uniquely Islamic sources. Granted that there are diverse opinions among Muslims concerning the precise direction such renewal should take, there is considerable agreement that the time is right for Muslims to act with renewed commitment to the mission of Islam: to command good and forbid evil; to strive to order society in a manner consistent with the guidance given to humanity by its creator. We may begin to understand the source and direction of that mission if we attend to the question, "What is Islam?" I propose, briefly, to consider three answers to that question. Islam is (1) the religious tradition that begins with the life and work of Muhammad, the Prophet of God; (2) the natural religion of all humanity; and (3) the driving force behind a great world civilization.

Muhammad, the Prophet of God

That Islam should be understood in connection with Muhammad the Prophet seems obvious.[8] The Muslim community begins with him; the story of his life, his call to prophecy, his career as prophet and statesman is basic to all Muslim piety. Here we can only provide the briefest sketch. According to tradition, Muhammad was born in 569 or 570 C.E. His father died before his birth; at age five or six, his mother also died. Muhammad was thus raised by his uncle, the man known as Abu Talib.

Abu Talib was a man of means; he was part of a merchant class that gained prominence as the result of the increased use of Mecca, a small city in the Arabian peninsula, as a center for trade during the middle of the sixth century. There were several trade routes that came through Mecca. In one way or another, all had the goal of fostering exchanges of goods between the great cities of the Byzantine empire (Damascus, Jerusalem) and India. Abu Talib and others like him made their fortunes by speculating on the profits to be made by the caravans transporting such goods.

That Abu Talib undertook to care for his nephew was according to the canons of the Arab tribal system dominant in the Arabian peninsula. The fundamental unit of that system was the clan, with its stipulation of the importance of duties of caring for one's "near kin" when they were in trouble. The clan formed the basis of the slightly looser association of the tribe; "Arab" society, such as it was, existed as a sort of recognition on the part of various tribes that they shared vague ancestral roots and honored some common notions of virtue. Such commonalities did not, however, lend themselves readily to ideas of national or ethnic identity. For that, the Arabs had to wait for the coming of Islam. The degree to which the Arab tribes were united and distinct can be shown with reference to the term *muruwwa*, "manliness." This term, more than others, signifies the code the tribes lived by.

Essentially, *muruwwa* raised to an ideal the virtues of a tribal chieftain. Manliness was shown in (1) bravery in battle; (2) generosity, especially to one's "clients" or the members of one's tribe; and (3) loyalty to the way (or *sunna*) set by ancestors of the tribe. Sexual prowess and the attainment of wealth were also part of the notion of *muruwwa*; in a sense, they "went along with" the one who was "manly." Most crucial to an understanding of the relationship that Islam would have to the *muruwwa* code are (1) certain limitations in the latter's scope—as a code inculcating loyalty to a particular tribe, it could not serve to turn mutual respect into nationhood; and (2) the relationship of *muruwwa* to religious relativism. Part of loyalty to the ancestral ways focused on the worship of tribal deities. At the time of Muhammad, the various tribal units had developed ways of respecting, even capitalizing on, the differences in piety that resulted.

Such differences in piety form an impressive part of the background of Muhammad's life in Mecca, the trading center of the Arabian peninsula. Muhammad's tribe, called Quraysh, traced its ancestry to the great men who had been given charge over the Kaᶜba (roughly, "cube") located just outside the city. One of those shrines which exist "time out of mind," the Kaᶜba seems to have been as old as Mecca itself—while Muhammad would eventually teach its construction by Abraham and his son, Ishmael, there does not seem to have been any tradition like this among the pre-Islamic Arab tribes. At the time of Muhammad's birth and his formative years, it seems clear that the Quraysh had, at least partly in the interests of trade, endeavored to make the Kaᶜba an ecumenical site. Thus came the tradition of a pilgrimage to Mecca, open to members of the various Arab tribes. The pilgrimage was made during certain agreed upon "truce months" in which no battles were to be fought, trade could occur, and the tribes could offer worship to their various deities. According to tradition, the Quraysh attempted to ensure that every tribe set up a replica of the favorite talisman of its deities in the Kaᶜba, to foster the universality of the shrine. From the Islamic point of view, this made the Kaᶜba a house of idols. It also served to emphasize the relative autonomy of and, subsequently, lack of communal feeling between the various tribes.

In this setting, Muhammad grew into a young man. We know little about his youth. Such stories as have come down serve to emphasize the idea that he was a person of good reputation, illustrating the noblest aspects of the Arab tribal code. At about age twenty-nine, he married Khadija, a widow several years older than Muhammad. Her wealth provided him with a new status in the community and also with time to pursue spiritual matters. Thus began a period of seeking, as Muhammad began to engage in extended periods of reflection and meditation. Again, we know little about his mind-set or what such seeking was intended to accomplish. Some scholars, building on such pieces of evidence as are available, place Muhammad in the context of a rather loose movement of Arabs who might be characterized as "unaffiliated monotheists." Dissatisfied with certain aspects of the Arab tribal code, yet not wanting to affiliate with "foreign" traditions like Christianity (identified largely with the Byzantine empire) or Judaism (Jewish Arab tribes in South Arabia had been accused of cooperating with the Sassanian empire), such people sought for an Arab monotheism. Such a faith would incorporate the best of the Arab tradition, yet provide it with a new, broader foundation on which the various tribes could become an *umma*—a transtribal community.

Whatever the case for this explanation of Muhammad's search, the notion of an Arab monotheism, equivalent to, yet distinct from, Christianity and Judaism, is an apt characterization of early Islam. At about forty years of age, Muhammad understood himself to be called to proclaim a message from God. All the traditional accounts emphasize that this call made him the prophet to the Arabs. He, like Moses and Jesus, had been given a particular mission within the providence of God: to proclaim God's word to a specific community—in Muhammad's case, those whose language was Arabic. And, like Moses and Jesus, Muhammad would receive a particular revelation to instruct, guide, and confirm his community in its mission: the Qurʾan, a scripture equivalent to the Torah and the Gospel, yet distinctly Arabic in language and tone.

According to Muslim tradition, the first verses of the Qurʾan were revealed to Muhammad in the year 610 C.E., during the month of Ramadan:

> Read: In the name of your Lord who creates,
> Creates humanity from a clot.
> Read: And your Lord is the Most Bounteous,
> Who teaches humanity by the pen,
> Teaches humanity that which it knew not.
>   (96:1–5)[9]

The rest of the book would be revealed periodically until 632 C.E., the year of Muhammad's death.

Muhammad's public ministry began shortly after his experience in 610 C.E. He began to proclaim the messages he received to the Quraysh, speaking to them about God, the moral law, and the day of judgment. While accounts of his early ministry report a certain degree of success, the overwhelming impression is of resistance to the Arab prophet—an impression that seems quite plausible, given the message Muhammad proclaimed. In short, he told his tribespeople that there was only one God (Allah); that the Kaʿba had been built originally for the worship of Allah, and that the practice of placing idols in it was wrong; that the city of Mecca had come to be dominated by people more interested in profits than justice; and that there would come a day when God would judge the citizens of Mecca (and indeed, all humanity) and requite them for their wrongdoing.

> Rivalry in worldly increase distracts you
> Until you come to the graves.
> Nay, but you will come to know!
> Nay, but you will come to know!
> Nay, would that you knew (now) with a sure knowledge!
> For you will behold hell-fire.
> Yes, you will behold it with sure vision.
> Then, on that day, you will be asked concerning pleasure.
>   (102)

Resistance to Muhammad reached a peak in the year 619 C.E., when Abu Talib and Khadija died. The death of the former left Muhammad without the protection that a prominent member of Quraysh could offer. Given the importance of tribal loyalties within the Arab system, this left Muhammad in a dangerous position. As to Khadija, it is enough to say that, in a society that allowed unlimited polygamy for men of means, Muhammad never took a second wife until after her death. Her death left him without an emotional base. Muhammad and his followers began to look for a new location, which was given to them by an invitation from the people of Yathrib, a city to the north of Mecca. Eventually called Medina, this became the city from which the Muslims would emerge as the most formidable military and political force in the Arabian peninsula.

The migration *(al-hijra)* to Medina took place in the year 622 C.E.—to the Muslims, the year 1. As the Muslims understood it, this change of location took place within the providence, even by the command, of God. It signified an important change in Muhammad's mission. According to the oldest extant Muslim biography of Muhammad, until the migration to Medina

> the apostle had not been given permission to fight or allowed to shed blood. . . . He had simply been ordered to call men to God and to endure insult and forgive the ignorant. The Quraysh had persecuted his followers, seducing some from their religion, and exiling others from their country. They had to choose whether to give up their religion, be maltreated at home, or to flee the country. . . .

> When Quraysh became insolent towards God and rejected His gracious purpose, accused His prophet of lying, and ill treated and exiled those who served Him and proclaimed His unity, believed in His prophet, and held fast to His religion, He gave permission to His apostle to fight and to protect himself against those who wronged them and treated them badly.

> The first verse which was sent down on this subject . . . was: "Permission is given to those who fight because they have been wronged. God is well able to help them,—those who have been driven out of their houses without right only because they said God is our Lord. Had not God used some men to keep back others, cloisters and churches and oratories and mosques wherein the name of God is constantly mentioned would have been destroyed. Assuredly God will help those who help Him."[10]

With the migration to Medina, Muhammad became not only a religious spokesman but a statesman and military leader. From its new location, the Muslim community conducted a military and political campaign that brought the Quraysh, and indeed the whole Arabian peninsula, to acknowledge the primacy of the Prophet. By the time of his death, Muhammad could say that "Arabia is solidly for Islam"; while the political reality of this would have to be reconfirmed and consolidated by Abu Bakr, first leader of the Muslims following Muhammad's death, the point of the saying is clear. The tribal system that dominated the Arabian peninsula at the time of Muhammad's birth had been transformed. A new kind of social and religious entity now existed. Where there had been the various tribes, each following the code of manliness according to its inherited piety, there was now the *umma muslima*, the "community of Muslims," with a shared faith based on the Qurʾan: There is no god but God, and Muhammad is God's messenger.

Islam, the Natural Religion

The narrative outlined above is crucial to understanding the source and direction of Islamic mission, not least in that it indicates a pattern to which all Muslims turn: the life of the Prophet, in which religion and statecraft, preaching and military action have a place. In his confrontation with the Arab tribal system, Muhammad perceived that his call was not "just to preach" but to reform and govern. In view of the circumstances, that required the use of force.

The Prophet's example is not only to be understood in the light of Arabian circumstances, however. It has universal significance. In the light of what has already been said, we should put it this way. Muhammad understood himself to be the Arab equivalent to Moses and Jesus. The Qurʾan presented itself as the distinctively Arabic version of that scripture previously revealed as Torah and Gospel. Yet, since the message of all prophets, as of all true scripture, is essentially the same, Muhammad and the Qurʾan embody a truth of broader import. Muhammad preached, and the Qurʾan contains a message about the natural religion of humanity. That religion, say the Muslims, is signified by the term *al-islam*, "the submission" to the will of God.

According to the Qurʾan, the rightness of this submission was established on the day of creation:

> And (remember) when your Lord brought forth from the Children
> of Adam, from their loins, their seed, and made them testify of
> themselves, (saying): Am I not your Lord? They said: Yes, truly. We

testify. (That was) lest you should say at the Day of Resurrection:
Lo! of this we were unaware.

(7:172)

All humanity knows the truth, that there is but one God, to whom we
owe obedience. Such knowledge exists as a kind of general revelation
that makes human beings accountable on the day of judgment.

The Qur'an goes on to say that, while the world is filled with
signs that point to the truth, human beings tend to ignore it. "Lo! We
offered the trust unto the heavens and the earth and the hills, but they
shrank from bearing it and were afraid of it. And human beings assumed it. Lo! They have proven to be tyrants and fools" (33:72). Human beings have the capacity to understand their duties to God and to
one another, if they would "reflect." But "rivalry in worldly increase"
distracts them; in other words, human beings spend their time and en-
ergy on the short-term goods available for this-worldly existence
rather than in taking stock of their position as creatures of God, made
to do God's will.

The knowledge available to human beings through general revelation, joined with the overwhelming tendency toward heedlessness, is
enough to justify God's judgment against them. In mercy, however,
God sends prophets, messengers whose task is to remind human beings of their duty. Speaking to people everywhere, in all places and
times, prophets have proclaimed the message: There is one God. There
is a right way to live. God will hold you accountable for your deeds,
according to the standard of right. Adam, Noah, Abraham, Isaac, Ja-
cob—all the great prophets of biblical lore are listed as proclaimers of
this message, as are other, less familiar names. Out of all the prophets,
however, three stand out: Moses, Jesus, Muhammad. Each of these not
only proclaimed the truth given to humanity on the day of creation;
each also brought a book that would give continual guidance and
founded a community intended to embody human submission to
God's will. Moses brought the Torah to the Jews; Jesus brought the
Gospel to the Christians; now Muhammad brings the Qur'an to the
Muslim community. In one sense, the religion of Moses and Jesus, as
well as of Muhammad, was Islam. In another sense, it would be up to
Muhammad and the Muslims to remind Jews and Christians of the
original message of the prophets.

Through his encounters with Jews and Christians, Muhammad
became convinced that these communities had forgotten that message:
that somehow, their rabbis and priests had misinterpreted the scriptures brought by Moses and Jesus. It became part of the mission of the
Muslims to remind Jews and Christians of true monotheism: the pure,

universal affirmation of the oneness of God that is part of the natural conscience of human beings everywhere. The Muslims, the Qur'an states, have been appointed as a "middle nation," to bear witness against the heedlessness of humankind. With respect to Jews and Christians, this involves affirmations like the following:

> [The Jews and Christians say,] None can enter Paradise unless he is a Jew or a Christian. These are their own desires. Say: Bring your proof (of what you state) if you are truthful. Nay, but who-ever surrenders his purpose to Allah while doing good, his re-ward is with his Lord; and there shall no fear come upon them, neither shall they grieve.
>
> And the Jews say the Christians follow nothing (true), and the Christians say the Jews follow nothing (true); yet both are readers of the Scripture. Even thus speak those who know not. Allah will judge between them on the Day of Resurrection concerning that wherein they differ....
>
> Unto Allah belong the East and the West, and whithersoever you turn, there is Allah's countenance. Lo! Allah is All-Embracing, All-Knowing.
>
> (2:111–115)

If the Muslims find their status, or, better, their mission, in the affirmation that their calling is to serve as a reminder to Jews and Christians of the original faith, then the Qur'an must also be understood in a slightly different light. Functionally, at least, it becomes more than an Arabic version of the Word of God, equivalent to Torah and Gospel. The Qur'an becomes the "decisive criterion," by which the monotheistic communities may resolve their religious disputes. In short, the best approximation to the pure monotheism natural to humanity is the religion established by Muhammad and the Qur'an: the religion of the *umma muslima*, the Muslim community.

Islam as a World Civilization

According to the Qur'an, all human beings are called to serve their creator; the knowledge of this duty is, in a sense, "imprinted" on their hearts. Prophecy only confirms and sharpens the general revelation available through reflection on the signs God has placed before us.

That being the case, Islam insisted from its inception that there are two choices available to human beings: to live in the way of *jahiliyya*, "heedlessness," for which the typical example was the pre-

Islamic Arabs; or to live in the way of *al-islam*, the submission to the will of God. The special vocation of the Muslim community is to bear witness to the latter choice and to show the excellence of Islam.

Within a generation after the Prophet's death, Muslims had attained political and military dominance over most of the territory now thought of as the Middle East. Eventually, most of the lands between Northern Africa and China (thinking east to west) or from India into south-central Europe (from south to north) came under one form or another of Islamic rule. The precise connection between the Islamic mission and the military campaigns that brought about this territorial expansion is a matter of some debate, to which we will return in the following chapter. That most Muslims thought of the spread of Islamic government as a blessing and responsibility, however, goes almost without saying.

In theory, submission to the will of God influences every aspect of human life. And in practice, one would have to look hard to find areas of interest to humanity in the regions already mentioned that did not interact with the basic worldview that Islam proclaimed: people came to associate certain patterns of governance, types of literature, philosophical positions, architectural designs, and especially modes of legal judgment with Islam. To what extent such patterns really flowed from Islam, as opposed to Islam giving its blessing to ways of thinking and ordering life that already existed in the conquered territories, is a matter very difficult to judge. That Muslims and others in these territories came to associate such patterns with the name "Islam," however, is beyond dispute. Especially during the era of the High Caliphate, identified with the reign of the Baghdad-based Abbasid dynasty (ca. 750–1258 C.E.), Islamic civilization was at the pinnacle of world power and influence.

It is this set of social, political, and intellectual practices that most Muslims think of when they speak of "Islamic civilization." In a sense, the period of the High Caliphate constitutes a golden age for Islam, so that one can speak of it as the "classical" period in Muslim history. Much contemporary Islamic writing looks back on this period with a certain nostalgia and wonders what would be necessary to restore Islam to its former influence.

We would be wrong, however, to understand the contemporary call for revival among Muslims as simple nostalgia. Even as some authors long for the glory of the past, others express a sense of betrayal or injustice in relation to the current status of Muslims in world affairs. Thus, observing the history of colonial and imperial rule in the traditionally Islamic lands over the last two centuries, writers and activists such as the Ayatullah Khumayni (Iran), Sayyid Qutb (Egypt), and

Abu'l A'la Mawdudi (Pakistan) have argued that the ascension of European and North American civilization in world affairs has been based on a failure of leadership in the Islamic world and on the Western willingness to shamelessly exploit, in the name of profit, the human and material resources of the developing countries. The mood of such writers is not nostalgia but outrage over the state of the world, in particular the state of the Muslim community.

Even rage, however, does not fully characterize the mood of Islamic revival and reform. For writers such as those listed, the tragedy of contemporary world affairs is that the Islamic voice cannot be heard; or, to put it another way, that the Muslim community lacks the power to carry out its mission of demonstrating to the world the excellence of pure monotheism. The problem is not just that the Muslims suffer indignity, or that traditionally Islamic countries are often weak and dependent on an alliance with the West to exercise influence. The problem is that human beings, created by God to do God's will, are missing the religious and moral guidance that a strong and flourishing Islamic community could provide. The call for renewal, then, relates to Islam and its mission. How shall it be carried out, in the context of present-day social and political realities?

Conclusion

We may refer once more to Saddam Hussein. Beginning with the fact that the Iraqi president attempted to manipulate symbols of the Islamic tradition in connection with the war in the Gulf, we have tried to understand the particular context in which such manipulation fits. When President Hussein placed the Gulf Crisis in the context of "the great crisis of this age in this great part of the world where the material side of life has surpassed the spiritual one and the moral one,"[11] he was speaking a language familiar to a people steeped in the idea that their community has a special place in the providential design of history. He spoke particularly to Arabs, tying such notions of mission to the fact that Islam, in a sense, began with the life and work of the Prophet sent to the Arabs and has always been identified with the Arabic scripture, the Qur'an. He also spoke to Muslims, Arabs or not, who would understand that the Muslim community is called to demonstrate the ways of monotheism to humanity.

However one thinks of Saddam Hussein, and whatever his ultimate fate will be, he can serve our inquiry in this respect. He reminds us, once again, of the importance of Islam in world affairs. The Gulf War was not just about oil, or markets, or even territory, pure and simple. It was a struggle over values; or more precisely, part of an ongoing struggle over who will define the direction and limits of appropriate political behavior in the modern world. When the Iraqi president described his confrontation with the West as a jihad, he was attempting to relate his particular political context to some of the most important values of the Arabic and Islamic cultural tradition. The extent of his success can be debated, as can the appropriateness of the attempt. Determining the latter, in particular, requires that we inquire further into Islamic approaches to the relationship of ethics, war, and statecraft. I propose to proceed with such inquiry, through an examination of the Islamic view of peace.

CHAPTER TWO

The Islamic View of Peace

There is, as is often noted, a tension in the term "peace." In one sense, the term signifies simply the absence of conflict. Religious and moral traditions, then, indicate concern for peace through proscriptions of the use of force, in particular lethal force.

On the other hand, peace may be taken as descriptive of an ideal state of affairs: the fruit of a just social order. In this connection, religious and moral traditions do not content themselves with proscriptions of force but hold out visions of a just society and encourage their adherents to strive for the fulfillment of same.

It was this second sense of peace that the late Paul Ramsey had in mind when he described the just war "doctrine" as the working "politico-military doctrine" of "the peoples of the West."[1] In particular, the just war tradition is the military portion of a theory of statecraft. It provides guidance concerning the place of force in the attempt to develop a just social order. In this way, just war tradition is connected with the desire to achieve and establish true peace. While Western culture is not without an interest in peace as the absence or avoidance of conflict, the emphasis on the connections between peace, order, and justice—and thus, on questions of the just use of force—has arguably been the stronger notion.

The Islamic tradition also presents evidence of both senses of peace. With respect to the desire to avoid conflict, one thinks of the Prophet's injunctions to avoid strife and wrongdoing. For example, in a sermon toward the end of his career, Muhammad said: "Know that every Muslim is a Muslim's brother, and that the Muslims are brethren. It is only lawful to take from a brother what he gives you willingly, so wrong not yourselves."[2]

29

Nevertheless, even a cursory reading of these texts indicates that such admonitions are set in the context of an interest in the achievement of an ideal social order. The connection of peace with justice is thus never far from the surface in Islam. It is Muslims who are "brothers"; they are to avoid conflict among themselves and those who enter into alliances with them. According to the famous Medina Constitution, which set the traditional pattern for relations between Muslims and Jews, among others: "Believers are friends one to the other to the exclusion of outsiders. To the Jew who follows us belong help and equality. He shall not be wronged nor shall his enemies be aided. The peace of believers is indivisible."[3]

In the fullest sense, peace is the product of order with justice. While one ought not despise the "peace of a sort" that comes from a simple avoidance of strife, one must always be aware that such a peace is uneasy and that conflict is always a possibility. In the Islamic tradition, then, one must strive for peace with justice. That is the obligation of believers; more than that, it is the natural obligation of all of humanity. The surest guarantee of peace is the predominance of al-islam, "the submission" to the will of God. One must therefore think in terms of an obligation to establish a social order in which the priority of Islam is recognized. But—and this is crucial—the submission that is the prerequisite of true peace is the fulfillment of humanity's true nature. Peace is the goal of life, justice the form of peace, an Islamic social order the security for all humanity within the providence of God, who placed guidance in the hearts of all creatures.

The Islamic view of peace is thus complex, even as is the Western view. The Islamic tradition stresses, not the simple avoidance of strife, but the struggle for a just social order. In its broadest sense, the Islamic view of peace, like its Western counterpart, is in fact part of a theory of statecraft founded on notions of God, of humanity, and of the relations between the two. This is most clear in connection with the development of the tradition by Sunni jurists during the classical period, and we begin our substantive examination of peace with their view. It is also necessary, however, to consider other viewpoints within the Islamic tradition; therefore we must spend some time discussing dissenting (in particular, Shiite) and reformist thought. In a third section of this chapter, I make some observations on the relationship of Western and Islamic views of peace before offering some concluding remarks.

The Classical View of Peace

The term "Sunni" designates the majority viewpoint in Islam. Emerging out of a long history of discussion concerning the proper understanding of Islamic approaches to theology, politics, and piety, the Sunni consensus came to be closely identified with the culture of the High Caliphate during the "classical" period of Islamic civilization.[4] Noting the intimate relations between Sunni intellectuals and political power during that period, some have characterized the Sunni approach as an apologia for the status quo—a kind of "establishment Islam." Such a description is not without merit; during the classical period, Sunni scholars were those most inclined to accept the world "as it is." In politics, for example, they took for granted the association of Islam with imperial power. Sunni writers, more than others, thought of the conquest of the Near East following the death of Muhammad in 632 C.E. as a just and natural extension of the work of the Prophet.

At the same time, the classical Sunni view of peace was developed by persons who were, so far as one can tell, devout and conscientious Muslims. Like others, they prayed to God: "Show us the straight path: The path of those whom you have favored; Not (the path) of those who earn your anger nor of those who go astray" (Qurʾan 1:6–7). Their understanding of politics, as of other aspects of life, involved the attempt to comprehend, in a systematic way, the guidance of God. That being the case, one might think of them as trying to work for the common good within the limits of a particular system rather than as apologists for the status quo. That is certainly how they thought of themselves.

The most characteristic way for Sunni intellectuals to think about peace (or, for that matter, about most moral and political issues) during the classical period was called al-fiqh. Literally indicating "the comprehension," fiqh came to be particularly associated with the attempt to make judgments consistent with al-shariʿa, usually translated as "Islamic religious law." The more straightforward meaning of al-shariʿa, however, has to do with the way of living that leads to Paradise. Al-fiqh, then, means the attempt to discover God's way, the "straight path" mentioned in the prayer quoted above.

Those intellectuals who specialized in this pursuit were called al-fuqaha, "those who comprehend." More prosaically, one could say that they were experts in analyzing human behavior in terms of a set of texts that Muslims agreed were authoritative for faith and practice. The Qurʾan, in particular, was the "speech" or word of God; collections of hadith or reports of Muhammad's words and deeds (his sunna or "customary practice") provided a second source of guidance. Sunni fuqaha felt these texts to be gifts of God, adequate sources to guide the whole of life. If problems occurred for which there was no direct guidance in the Qurʾan or the approved collections of hadith, then scholars engaged in various types of reasoning, the most characteristic being qiyas or a type of reasoning by making an analogy from precedents found in the authoritative texts. Overall, the endeavor to comprehend God's guidance was governed by the notion that consensus was authoritative. For most, this meant that the consensus of scholars on a particular judgment served to check idiosyncratic appropriations of Qur'an and *hadith*. God would never allow God's people to live in error. Through the process of discussing human affairs in the light of revealed texts, human beings would eventually discover the proper course to take.

With respect to the nature of peace, the combination of an established political entity that was, at least in principle, Islamic and the desire systematically to comprehend the guidance of God led to the elaboration of a kind of "law of nations" *(al-siyar)*. Theoretically this law was to govern the relations between the Islamic state and all others. The classical, Sunni view of peace was thus set in the context of a general theory of statecraft that presupposed certain political realities and that was also informed by a particular interpretation of sources considered authoritative in matters of human conduct. The central components of this perspective can be outlined as follows.

First, there was a conception of human responsibility. As seen in chapter 1, the Qur'an indicates that all human beings are accountable to the one God, who is their creator. They are so, not first of all because God has addressed them through prophecy—a kind of special revelation. From the beginning, human beings were endowed with a knowledge that makes them responsible beings. This is the import of a number of verses in the Qur'an, among which the following are the most famous:

> And (remember) when your Lord brought forth from the Children
> of Adam, from their loins, their seed, and made them testify of
> themselves, (saying): Am I not your Lord? They said: Yes, truly.
> We testify. (That was) lest you should say at the Day of Resurrec-
> tion: Lo! of this we were unaware. Or lest you should say: (It is)
> only (that) our fathers ascribed partners to Allah of old and were
> (their) seed after them. Will You destroy us on account of that
> which those who follow falsehood did?
>
> (7:172–173)

One is reminded of the Pauline affirmation: "For since the creation of the world [God's] invisible attributes, His eternal power and divine nature, have been clearly seen, being understood through what has been made, so that [human beings] are without excuse" (Rom. 1:20). The import is much the same: the responsibility of humanity, that which deprives human beings of an "excuse" on judgment day, is established by a knowledge "written on their hearts" by God. Classical

Sunni thinkers disagreed among themselves on the precise content of this knowledge. Did it include the first principles of morality (for example), or only the knowledge necessary to recognize true revelation? No one denied the existence of such a "prior" or "general" revelation as the presupposition of human responsibility before God, however.

Second, there was a judgment about the human situation. On this point, the Sunni position simply followed the Qurʾan. There is a problem with humanity which, simply put, is that human beings forget or ignore the guidance written on their hearts by God. In view of this situation, it is an act of mercy that God continues to sustain humanity. Yet God does this, and even more sends the prophets who remind humanity of its responsibility. The special revelation given through prophets and in scriptures does not contradict but confirms, extends, and reinforces the natural guidance given to all humanity.

The message of the prophets sets in stark relief the two choices available to humanity: the way of heedlessness or ignorance (al-jahiliyya), by which the quest for "worldly increase" leads to ever-deeper religious and moral error; and the way of submission (al-islam), by which human beings adhere to the Qurʾan's admonition:

> So set your purpose ... for religion as one by nature upright—the
> nature (framed) by Allah, in which He has created humanity.
>
> (30:30)

The way of heedlessness exemplifies and furthers a kind of "sickness of the heart" (2:10) by which human beings increasingly live in that state of nature described by Thomas Hobbes as "solitary, poor, nasty, brutish, and short." The way of submission, by contrast, leads to peace in connection with a just social order.

Third, there was a political application of this judgment. The way of heedlessness and the way of submission are seen as institutionalized in the existence of Islamic and non-Islamic political entities. The former may be described as the territory of Islam (dar al-islam); the latter is the territory of war (dar al-harb). The territory of Islam signifies a political entity that acknowledges the supremacy of Islamic values. In the Sunni view, this means either (a) the ruler is knowledgeable in and capable of making judgments on the basis of the Qurʾan and hadith; (b) the ruler, who is primarily a political figure, nevertheless consults with religious scholars on matters of policy; or (c) the ruler at least gives lip service to Islamic values and does not command anything directly opposed to the consensus of the scholars. In general, it is the religious affiliation of the head of state that is crucial. The people of the territory of Islam need not all be Muslims. The Sunni view of peace explicitly provides for religious pluralism through the notion of "protected" religious groups (called *dhimmiyya*) who enjoy relative freedom so long as they pay tribute and thus acknowledge Islamic sovereignty.

The territory of Islam is theoretically the territory of peace and justice. One ought to emphasize "theoretically"; the Sunni theorists were quite realistic about the limitations of human political action. Their point, however, was that the establishment of a political entity that acknowledges Islam provides the best and most secure peace available to humanity. This is so because such an entity provides the closest approximation to the natural capacities of human beings.

By contrast, the territory of war is the epitome of human heedlessness and ignorance. It is characterized by disorder and internal strife; it also constitutes a continual threat to the security of the territory of Islam. The disorder can be mitigated, of course, as can the threat to Islamic values, if some portion of the territory of war is governed by a scriptural religion such as Christianity. But even this arrangement causes difficulties, since "actual" Christianity does not correspond to the true religion of Jesus. The peace of the world cannot be *fully* secure unless all people come under the protection of an Islamic state. Thus there always exists an imperative for Muslims: to struggle to extend the boundaries of the territory of Islam. This is the Muslim way—the "natural" way—to fulfill the trust given to humanity by its creator: to establish peace with justice within a secure political order.

Thus, fourth, the classical Sunni perspective on peace involved a program of action. The struggle to extend the boundaries of the territory of Islam is the jihad (literally, "struggle" or "effort"). It is a struggle that takes place at the intersection of heedlessness and submission; more concretely, the Sunni theorists thought of jihad as the form of Islamic action at the intersection of the territory of Islam and the territory of war.

It is crucial in this context to understand the polyvalence of the term "jihad." It does not always mean "holy war," or even "war." The struggle to extend the boundaries of the territory of Islam, and thus to extend the influence of Islamic values, takes place in a number of ways. A saying attributed to the Prophet illustrates this: "It is the duty of every Muslim to command the good and forbid the evil with the heart, the tongue, and the hand (or sword)." According to Islamic tradition, the "great jihad" is the struggle with one's own heart, the attempt to bring oneself into accord with the will of God. The means appropriate to this struggle are prayer, study, and various forms of action reminiscent of what Max Weber called inner-worldly asceticism. In some sense, this is a point of consistency; it makes little sense to claim status as a *mujahid*, struggling to bring guidance to the world, if there is no corresponding growth in one's own awareness of God.

Struggle with the tongue implies missionary endeavor. The proclamation of the oneness of God, the coming judgment, and the necessity of living according to true guidance are the preferred means of carrying out the struggle to extend the territory of Islam. "There is no compulsion in religion," says the Qur'an (2:256). No one should make converts by the sword; unwilling faith is insincere, almost by definition. Despite its reputation, the Islamic tradition knew this as well as any other and distinguished the ideal of faith *(al-iman)* from the practice of submission *(al-islam)*. Indeed, one form of the Prophetic saying cited above continues to demonstrate the priority of missionary endeavor in the spread of Islamic values. Rather than proceeding from the jihad of the tongue to the sword, this form moves from the tongue to the pen—thus stressing the propagation of the Islamic message in an attempt to persuade persons to adhere to the natural religion of humanity.

In the end, however, Sunni theorists understood force to be a possible and useful means of extending the territory of Islam and thus a tool in the quest for peace. While force should never be the first resort, it could be justified under certain conditions. This leads to a discussion of the rules governing armed conflict.

1. There must be a just cause—viz., the imperative to extend the boundaries of the territory of Islam. But this is not enough, in and of itself, for the preferred means to fulfill this imperative is through the proclamation of true guidance and the persuasion of all humanity to walk in the "straight path." Something additional is necessary if the use of lethal force is to be justified. For a number of Sunni theorists, this "something" is the refusal of a non-Islamic political entity to acknowledge the sovereignty of Islam through the rulers converting to Islam or through the payment of tribute. This refusal is made plain in connection with

2. An invitation/declaration of Muslim intentions. The ruler of the Muslims is to communicate with enemy authorities, inviting them to accept Islam in one of two ways: either they must become Muslims or they must agree to pay tribute as an acknowledgment of the authority of the Islamic state. This invitation is accompanied by a declaration of the resolve of the Muslims to fight, should the enemy refuse the invitation.

3. Already implicit is a requirement of right authority. It is not individual Muslims who declare the intention of their community to fight, should the invitation to accept Islam be refused. It is the head of the Islamic state. That person is responsible to assess the military capacity of the Muslims, to weigh the probabilities of success, and to assure formal adherence to the procedures outlined in item 1. To ensure that the jihad is carried out by missionary and/or military activity is the

same person's special obligation in the Muslim community. Correspondingly, it is the obligation of ablebodied, adult Muslim males who have no outstanding debts to answer the summons of their leader, should he call upon them to participate in the jihad.

4. The war must be conducted in accordance with Islamic values. The meaning of this requirement will be discussed in greater detail in subsequent chapters. For now, it suffices to say that the Muslim forces are supposed to fight with right intent: not primarily for the spoils of war, not for personal glory, but for the cause and in the path of God. Their aim is to be the promotion of those values which make for peace. They are to discriminate between the guilty and the innocent as they attack enemy targets, and they are to use the minimum force required for victory. Not that Sunni theorists were shy about the destructive power of war. On this point they were quite realistic: if it is important to fight, then it is important to win. And, if strategic considerations lead to actions that appear to violate the rules of war, then the necessity of winning provides an excusing condition for the Muslim armies. Indeed, one could say that the fault for excessive enemy casualties devolves upon the enemy leaders. It is the recalcitrance of such leaders in the face of truth that has led to suffering for their people.

The formal parallels between these rules of war and the Western just war criteria are rather striking. Just cause, right intent, competent authority, a reasonable hope of success, the aim of peace—all these criteria of the *jus ad bellum* are formally present in the rules governing jihad, as is the *jus in bello* requirement for discrimination in targeting. At the same time, some criteria either do not appear or have a rather different content than just war thinkers are wont to provide. The *jus ad bellum* proportionality, for example, is present mainly as a type of prudential reasoning on the part of the authorities concerning the strength of the Muslim forces over against their enemies. The requirement of an invitation/declaration of Muslim intentions, while it indicates that war is not the preferred means of carrying out the struggle to extend the influence of Islamic values, is not the same as the just war tradition's "last resort." And just cause appears to have a religious content that just war thinking, at least in its modern forms, desires to avoid. We shall return to these and other considerations toward the end of this chapter.

Shiite and Reformist Views

At this point, however, it is important to note that the perspective developed by Sunni scholars during the classical period of Islam is not all there is to the Islamic view of peace. Even during the classical period there was a minority perspective associated with the various

Shiite groups. The most important of these for our purposes is the Twelvers, prominent especially in Iran.

The great divide between the Twelver Shiite scholars and those associated with the Sunni tradition has always been a dispute concerning the leadership of the Islamic community. Disagreement on this point is associated with a number of other differences, not least concerning the doctrine of God, the nature of the Qurʾan, the relationship between God's power and human responsibility, and the identification of a true Muslim. But for our purposes, the leadership issue is the key.

All of the groups associated with the name "Shiʿa" held a version of the following belief. In each generation, God appoints a righteous person who is the one truly legitimate leader for the Muslim community— really, of all humanity. Muhammad was such a person, distinguished by the joining of his leadership with the vocation of a prophet, so that he not only provided political leadership but brought a revelation reminding humanity of true guidance and founded the Muslim community. Prophecy stops with Muhammad, from the Shiite point of view. But the need of the Muslims, and of humanity, for leadership does not. A just God will not leave humanity without a "proof" (al-hujja) of the divine intention to establish peace in the context of a just social order. And so God appointed a leader (al-imam) to succeed Muhammad; this was Ali, son-in-law of the Prophet. The sign of God's appointment, for Ali and those who would follow him, is the "designation" (al-nass) provided by the previous leader—in Ali's case, Muhammad. With such designation, the divinely appointed leader is effectively set apart. He is safeguarded by God from the commission of any grave sins, and it is the obligation of all humanity to recognize and follow him. At his direction, the Muslims carry out the jihad, which has the purpose of extending his rule, or of extending the territory of Islam (which is in effect the same thing).

The difficulty for much of Shiite thought was that most of the imams were unable to achieve success in this world—a fact that gives a peculiar flavor to Shiite perceptions of the historic development of the Islamic community. In particular, the Shiites could not act as apologists for the seventh-century conquests that formed the territorial basis for the High Caliphate. For the most part, the military efforts associated with this political entity, so important in the development of Sunni thought, were regarded by the Shiites as illegitimate. Viewed as usurpers of the right to rule, the Sunni caliphs could not be considered legitimate guides for the struggle to extend Islamic territory. In terms of the rules of war, the efforts of such caliphs suffered from one fatal flaw: they did not, and could not, satisfy the criterion of right authority.

This general difficulty became critical for the Twelvers beginning in 874 C.E., the beginning of (what is termed) the occultation of the Twelfth Imam. The infant son of Hasan al-Askari (d. 873/74), whose name was Muhammad, disappeared around the time of his father's death. The extremely complex traditions surrounding this event and the subsequent development of the Twelver Shiite doctrine of Muhammad, son of Hasan al-Askari as *al-mahdi*, the rightly guided one who would one day appear to lead the Muslim community in a victorious effort to establish peace with justice, have been carefully studied by others.[5] With respect to the topic of this chapter, the critical point is the problem created for Shiite political thought by the occultation of the Twelfth Imam. How could (can) there be a jihad, especially a jihad involving resort to war, in the absence of the divinely appointed leader? The answer is, in a sense, that there cannot be. At least, there can be no jihad in the sense envisioned by the Sunni theorists. Following the disappearance of the Twelfth Imam, the Twelver Shiites affiliated with a variety of political regimes in the general region of Iran: the Buyids (932–1055); the Safavids (1502–1779); the Qajars (1779–1914); and the Pahlavis (1926–1978/79). The Shiite association with such regimes was justified as a kind of interim measure: there must be some form of political order until the Imam appears, said the Shiite scholars. Given the available choices, it is desirable to have an order that at least acknowledges the priority of Shiite Islam and in which the established authority consults with Shiite religious leaders on matters of policy. What was not given (and could not be given) to such regimes was permission to use armed force to extend the territory of Islam.

Thus the only use of lethal force that the Shiite religious scholars would grant as legitimate for their "interim regimes" was the defensive use. Such defensive wars could be classified as jihad, in the sense that there is an expenditure of effort in the path of God, in particular for the sake of defending Islamic (Shiite) territory. Properly, however, such wars are not jihad, but *defaꞌ*: wars "imposed" on the Islamic community by hostile and aggressive political forces. According to Abdulaziz Sachedina, the notion of defensive wars was developed rather extensively by Shiite jurists, so that one may think of a spectrum of defensive wars.[6] At one end of the spectrum are those wars imposed by an actual attack. At the other end are those in which a community responds to some impending danger through a preemptive strike.

This background is crucial to an understanding of the career of the late Ayatullah Khumayni, the occurrence of the Iranian Revolution and subsequent formation of the Islamic Republic of Iran, and of Iran's conduct in its long war with Iraq during the 1980s. In so many ways, Khumayni's political thought and speeches indicate the perception that Muhammad Reza Shah, last (at this point) of the Pahlavi rulers, had violated the trust given him by the people of Iran. Khumayni held that, in the light of this violation, it was the assigned task of the Shiite scholars, as guardians of Islam in the absence of the Twelfth Imam, to defend Islam by overthrowing the Shah. The Shah is accused by Khumayni of allowing the United States to conduct a hostile takeover of Iran. The Shah is charged with making war on Islam rather than defending it. The revolution of 1978/79 is thus justified.[7]

Similarly, the formation of an Islamic republic is justified. In the absence of the Twelfth Imam, no society can be perfectly just. Specifically, there are limits on the actions that a Shiite state may undertake to achieve justice and peace. But it is the responsibility of religious scholars to ensure the relative justice of a Shiite state and to strive with all legitimate means to propagate Islamic values. The jihad of the heart and the tongue are appropriate, even when the jihad of the sword is not. This is the implication of statements such as the following:

> We [Iran] have repeatedly shown in our foreign and international policy that we have been and are intent on expanding the influence of Islam in the world and lessening the domination of the world devourers. Now, if the servants of the United States cite this policy as being expansionist and motivated to establish a great empire, we will not fear it but welcome it. . . . We are intent on tearing out the roots of corrupting Zionism, Capitalism, and Communism in the world. We have decided to rely on God Almighty to destroy the regimes which are based on these three pillars, in order to spread the regime of the messenger of God.[8]

Finally, the war with Iraq was justified as *defaᶜ*, meaning that it qualified as a war in defense of Islamic territory. Iranian soldiers, Khumayni said, were protecting Islamic territory and values; Iraqi soldiers, misled by President Saddam Hussein, were fighting against their own religion.

The importance of the Shiite background in the war with Iraq is seen in the fact that Iran never officially declared its defense a jihad. The war was *defaᶜ*, imposed by the rebellious Iraqi regime. At least in the early going, Iran indicated its desire to distinguish the Iraqi populace from the regime of Saddam Hussein and to conduct the war according to Islamic principles. Iran held to a policy consistent with this position into 1984, in contrast with the Iraqi policy of deliberately targeting civilians in an effort to diminish popular support for the war among Iranian citizens. Eventually, Iran did engage in some attacks on Iraqi cities as a means of indicating its determination in the war. It does not seem, however, that the Islamic Republic ever waged counterpopulation war to the extent that Iraq did.

In terms of the classical heritage of Islam, the Shiite stress on the limits placed on the struggle to extend Islamic values (by the heart and the tongue, but not by the sword) represents a dissenting perspective, especially with respect to the place of armed conflict in the Islamic mission. Yet it is interesting to note that Sunni thought has, in modern times, developed in ways that present striking parallels to the Shiite position. It is fairly common for Sunni "modernists" to argue that the Qurʾan's teaching on jihad allows for the use of military force only in the case of a defense of Islamic territory or values. The treatise of Mahmud Shaltut on *The Koran and Fighting* (originally published in 1948), for example, presents the thought of a formidable Sunni scholar, eventually the Shaykh al-Azhar, the leading spokesman for "establishment Islam" in Egypt.[9] Shaltut's tract is clearly apologetic in nature, but it nevertheless makes a powerful case for an interpretation of the Qurʾan verses on fighting that focuses on the defense of the Islamic community. Fighting cannot be an essential part of the Islamic mission, argues Shaltut, for the heart of Muhammad's mission is to bring good tidings and to warn humanity. That being the case, the mission of the Muslim community focuses on persuasion. Fighting is justified only in cases of defense, which Shaltut identifies with efforts "to stop aggression, to protect the Mission of Islam, and to defend religious freedom."[10]

When compared with the classical Sunni perspective, Shaltut is obviously a reformer. He gives the Qurʾan verses priority over the consensus of his Sunni forebears and thus reaches a different conclusion about the place of armed force in the quest for peace with justice.

A somewhat different perspective is presented by other contemporary Sunni texts, usually identified as militant or fundamentalist. *The Neglected Duty*, for example, advertised as the "Creed of Sadat's Assassins," argues vigorously for armed struggle against rulers who, while ostensibly Muslim, refuse to implement a government based on Islamic values.[11] We shall return to this text in chapter 5, in connection with a discussion of irregular war.

Comparative Observations

From the standpoint of comparative religious ethics, it is important to consider the relationship between the Islamic view of peace and predominant Western views. A number of the most significant issues have to do with the place of war in the quest for peace.

First, there are issues connected with the question, What constitutes a just cause for war? The classical Sunni view makes religion a legitimate cause of war, not in the sense of the use of force in direct attempts to convert persons to Islam, but in the sense of extending the geographic boundaries of the territory of Islam. The Shiite view restricts the expansionist dimensions of the Sunni perspective, as do at least some of the reformist Sunni views. Even those who stress that only defensive wars are justified are still thinking in terms of the defense of religion, however; more precisely, they are thinking in terms of the defense of a political entity identified with Islamic values. By way of comparison, just war tradition has, at least since the seventeenth century, insisted that "difference in religion is not a just cause of war." Contemporary just war discussion tends, with a few exceptions, to be conducted on the assumption that wars are more humane when religion is left out.

A second set of issues emerges when one considers the conduct of war. Modern just war thinking tends to make *jus in bello* restraints *the* test of justice in war. We cannot always tell, the reasoning goes, which side truly has a just cause. International politics is too complicated for that; while one might suppose that historical inquiry will ultimately vindicate one side or the other, the truth of the matter is that both sides may have some degree of right on their side. In this regard, just war thinkers developed the notion of simultaneous ostensible justice, which allows for the appearance, at least, of a war between forces that are morally equivalent.

In such cases, modern just war thought argues that the real test of justice has to do with how fighting forces deal with the *jus in bello* requirements of proportionality and discrimination. How seriously do the opposing sides attempt to honor (a) the principle that the amount of force used must be proportionate to the goal sought; and (b) the requirement that noncombatants must never be the target of direct military action?

Prima facie, the Islamic tradition speaks to these concerns. As indicated, Sunni theorists developed their *jus in bello* thought around the notion that a jihad must be fought according to Islamic values. These include something like the just war notions of proportionality and discrimination. How much the two traditions resemble each other at this point needs further inquiry, particularly in the light of the special concerns raised by modern weaponry. How do Islamic thinkers deal with questions about the potential and/or actual use of weapons of mass destruction?

Third, there are issues connected with the various kinds of conflict that just war thinkers describe as "irregular." Especially in view of the contemporary phenomenon of "fundamentalist" or "militant" Islam, it seems appropriate to ask, What does the Islamic tradition say about military action on the part of individual citizens, militia groups—in a phrase, "soldiers without portfolio"? Historically, just war tradition dealt very harshly with the perpetrators of such action, characterizing them as little more than brigands. Contemporary just war thinking is more favorably disposed. Yet important issues remain: in view of the requirement that wars be authorized by a competent authority, how can irregulars be said to fight a just war? That is not to mention the *jus in bello* problems posed by kidnapping, assassination, terrorism, and other tactics often associated with irregular wars.

From the preceding discussion, it would seem that Islam has similar problems. For Sunni and Shiite theorists, jihad requires the presence of competent or right authority. Indeed, the major division between such theorists on matters of war has to do with how such authority is constituted. *Jus in bello* concerns are not without import as well.

Conclusion

These three sets of issues constitute points for discussion between the Western tradition of the just war and the Islamic traditions concerning jihad. In subsequent chapters, we shall take up each of them in turn.

In all such inquiry, however, one should not lose sight of the connections between notions of justice in war and the aim of peace. This chapter has argued that the Islamic discussion of jihad has its proper place in the context of Islamic notions of mission. To put it another way, the "jihad tradition," as just war thought, is the special military aspect of a "working politico-military doctrine" by which Muslims attempt to foster stable relations between peace, order, and justice in human affairs. As we engage in comparisons of the Islamic approach to the justification and limitation of war, we must keep in mind the notion of mission characteristic of all Islamic tradition: to demonstrate to the world the values associated with pure monotheism; to command good, forbid evil, and bring about justice in the earth.

I close with this anecdote. Some years ago a student asked me, "Do you think the Islamic State is here to stay?" He meant the state as represented in Iran. In that sense, the answer is, "I don't know." But if we alter the question slightly, to indicate concern with the phenomenon of political Islam, the answer is clearly "Yes." For, as the examples I have given indicate, Islam is by its nature interested in politics. It is, by tradition and historic experience, interested in the creation and preservation of a political entity that in some sense reflects Islamic values. It is, to put it another way, interested not just in the avoidance of conflict but in the creation of a just society. That, I think, is the conclusion to which a consideration of the Islamic view of peace leads.

CHAPTER THREE

Religion as a Cause of War: Resort to War in the Islamic Tradition

Commenting on the extremely complex and varied relations that occur between the phenomena he called "exemplary" and "ethical" prophecy, Max Weber says the following:

> Neither religion nor men are open books. They have been historical rather than logical or even psychological constructions without contradiction. Often they have borne within themselves a series of motives, each of which, if separately and consistently followed through, would have stood in the way of the others or run against them head-on. In religious matters "consistency" has been the exception and not the rule.[1]

We do well to remember Weber's comment in studying the relationship of religion and war. For there seems to be a very great temptation to simplify that relation. Much contemporary just war thinking, in particular, proceeds on the assumption that the logic of "wars of religion" or "holy wars" is such that the conception of religion as a *casus belli* leads ineluctably to the disintegration of standards of discrimination and proportionality. In short, we are told that when resort to war is governed by religion, limitation of war takes a back seat. With respect to the Christian tradition, this is the line suggested by Roland Bainton in his classic *Christian Attitudes Toward War and Peace*.[2] In short, Bainton argued that just war thinking emerged as a kind of antidote to wars of religion; that one of the identifying characteristics of the just war tradition is its limitation of just cause to secular motivations such as the defense of national boundaries; and that this secularization of war led to

more humane conceptions concerning the ways wars ought to be conducted.

Despite criticism from scholars of considerable renown, Bainton's account still weighs deeply on the minds of just war theorists.[3]
This is the reason why, we are told, it is so important that the just war
tradition teaches us to limit resort to war to moral and political causes.
Resort to and limitation of war are linked—if we can reserve the *jus ad
bellum* to secular causes, we can preserve the humanitarian aims of the
jus in bello.

In a widely discussed article in the *Atlantic Monthly*, the noted Is-
lamicist Bernard Lewis appears to take the same line with respect to
conceptions of war in Islam. Lewis writes:

> In Islam the struggle of good and evil very soon acquired political
> and even military dimensions. Muhammad, it will be recalled,
> was not only a prophet and a teacher, like the founders of other
> religions; he was also the head of a polity and of a community, a
> ruler and a soldier. Hence his struggle involved a state and its
> armed forces. If the fighters in the war for Islam, the holy war "in
> the path of God," are fighting for God, it follows that their oppo-
> nents are fighting against God. And since God is in principle the
> sovereign, the supreme head of the Islamic state—and the Prophet
> and, after the Prophet, the caliphs are his viceregents—then God
> as sovereign commands the army. The army is God's army and
> the enemy is God's enemy. The duty of God's soldiers is to dis-
> patch God's enemies as quickly as possible to the place where
> God will chastise them—that is to say, the afterlife.[4]

As an exercise in logic, insistent that a particular *telos* follows
from the consistent application of certain notions of religious and political authority, this analysis may suffice. As a piece of history, it will not.
For the record of Islamic conceptions of war and statecraft indicates a
way of thinking far more subtle, and with greater nuance, than Lewis's
comments allow. Space does not allow for an engagement of all the issues raised in Lewis's essay. In this chapter, I shall focus on issues connected with the last two lines of the quotation: "The army is God's
army and the enemy is God's enemy. The duty of God's soldiers is to
dispatch God's enemies as quickly as possible to the place where God
will chastise them—that is to say, the afterlife." I shall argue the following case: The Islamic tradition, in both classical and contemporary
manifestations, suggests that, contrary to Lewis's depiction, the idea of
religion as a *casus belli* provides a way to *limit* the occasion and the
damage of war. In short, the Islamic tradition suggests that "holy war"

is *not* the equivalent of "total war," any more than "just war" always means "limited war." As an exercise in comparative religious ethics, an engagement with the tradition of Islam suggests that the relations between resort to and limitation of war *are* closely connected, but not in the ways that many of us trained in contemporary just war thinking have learned.

Examples from Classical Islam

We can begin with some examples from the classical period of Islamic civilization, ca. 750–1258 C.E. Identified in previous chapters with the period of the Abbasid caliphate, classical Islam developed its conceptions of war, as of other aspects of human affairs, in the context of an imperial state, based in Baghdad and governing territories from the Nile to the Oxus. This was the great period of Islamic intellectual and cultural development, including the two great forms of Islamic piety: those of the Sunni and the Shiᶜa. We have seen that each presents a distinctive way of thinking about resort to and limitation of war. Each builds on the notion, exemplified by Muhammad and ensconced in the Qurʾan, that war is at times a necessity in the world of human beings. As the Qurʾan puts it:

> Warfare is ordained for you, though it is hateful unto you; but it may happen that you hate a thing which is good for you, and it may happen that you love a thing which is bad for you. Allah knows, you know not.   (2:216)

> Sanction is given unto those who fight because they have been wronged; and Allah is indeed able to give them victory; Those who have been driven from their homes unjustly only because they said: Our Lord is Allah—For had it not been for Allah's repelling some men by means of others, cloisters and churches and oratories and mosques, wherein the name of Allah is oft mentioned, would assuredly have been pulled down. Truly Allah helps one who helps Him. Lo! Allah is Strong, Almighty.   (22:39–40)

As the Muslims understood it, Muhammad's military campaigns against the Meccans had merely been the outworking of such notions. It was part of his obedience to the dictate to "enjoin right conduct and forbid indecency" (3:104) or to "make God's cause succeed" (8:39).[5] At least with respect to the example of Muhammad, then, it was possible to speak of use of lethal force which was right, in the sense of divinely sanctioned—even, divinely commanded.[6]

Classical Islamic thought took this as a given. Thus in one sense pacifism, in the sense of a thoroughgoing rejection of war, was not an option for Muslim thinkers. That did not mean, however, that such thinkers accepted war as the normal condition of humanity. Rather, the Qur'an and the example of Muhammad gave them a means by which to discriminate between legitimate and illegitimate uses of force.

For the Sunni theorists, representing the majority, war had been a means for the establishment of an Islamic state, in which the ruler was a Muslim who (theoretically) consulted with Islamic authorities on matters of policy. This state they called the *dar al-islam*—"territory of Islam," or, to play out their meaning, "the territory where justice and peace are possible." The wars fought by Muhammad, and by those Muslim rulers who were "rightly guided," had as their purpose "to make God's cause succeed"—to bring the world under the sway of God's guidance and to lead humanity in the way of peace. The point was *not* to make converts. It was to establish the rule of God. These kinds of war—and these only—could be connected with the symbol of jihad—the "struggle" to implement the will of God. For other kinds of war, the preferred term was *harb*, a generic term that signified wars fought for less glorious and less approved purposes.

With respect to the interests of this chapter, it is important to note already the role of religion in limiting war. For the Sunni theorists, "just war" was limited to jihad, that is, to war that could be identified with obedience to God's command to "command good and forbid evil," to establish peace and justice on the earth. Further, a war "in the path of God," fought according to God's purposes, should also be fought according to God's design. Thus the literature of the classical period features prominently the following report *(hadith)* concerning the custom of Muhammad:

> Whenever the Apostle of God sent forth an army or a detachment, he charged its commander personally to fear God, the Most High, and he enjoined the Muslims who were with him to do good [i.e., to conduct themselves properly].

> And [the Apostle] said:

> Fight in the name of God and in the "path of God" [i.e., truth]. Combat [only] those who disbelieve in God. Do not cheat or commit treachery, nor should you mutilate anyone or kill children. Whenever you meet your polytheist enemies, invite them [first] to adopt Islam. If they do so, accept it, and let them alone. You should then invite them to move from their territory to the territory of the

émigrés [Madina]. If they do so, accept it and let them alone. Otherwise, they should be informed that they would be [treated] like
the Muslim nomads (Bedouins) [who take no part in the war] in
that they are subject to God's orders as [other] Muslims, but that
they will receive no share in either the ghanima (spoil of war) or
in the *fay*. If they refuse [to accept Islam], then call upon them to
pay the jizya (poll tax); if they do, accept it and leave them alone.
If you besiege the inhabitants of a fortress or a town and they try
to get you to let them surrender on the basis of God's judgment,
do not do so, since you do not know what God's judgment is, but
make them surrender to your judgment and then decide their case
according to your own views. But if the besieged inhabitants of a
fortress or a town asked you to give them a pledge [of security] in
God's name or in the name of His Apostle, you should not do so,
but give the pledge in your names or in the names of your fathers;
for, if you should ever break it, it would be an easier matter if it
were in the names of you or your fathers.[7]

Other traditions have the Prophet establishing proper conditions
for the distribution of booty, the duties of various classes of Muslims
to participate in war, vesting the leader of the Muslims with authority
to determine the appropriate time to fight, indicating the acceptable
terms of treaties of peace, and indicating certain categories of enemy
persons who are "restricted" targets.

These considerations suggest a second way that religion serves to
limit war. From the Sunni perspective, the religious aims of the jihad
impose a certain set of means. The religious limitation of war is not
only "at the front end," with respect to the *jus ad bellum*, where jihad is
distinguished from *harb*. It is also present "at the back end," with respect to the *jus in bello*. Notions of proper conduct in war follow from
the religious purposes of jihad. The precise relationship of the Islamic
jus in bello to the just war tradition needs further exploration. It may be
that just war thinkers find the Muslim ways of implementing concerns
for proportionality and discrimination less than adequate—we shall
have to see. But the central fact—that in the case of Sunni thought, religion is conceived as a *limit* on war—seems to me to be incontrovertible.

In the same vein, we must consider Shiite thought. With the Sunnis, the Shiites considered religion the only legitimate cause for war.
Under the right conditions, Shiite scholars argued that war could be a
legitimate way to "make God's cause succeed." But the historical experience of the Shiites was different from the Sunnis'; as a minority, often
persecuted by the Imperial State, the Shiites were less inclined than the
Sunnis to assign the label "jihad" to wars conducted by the existing

authorities. Among the Twelvers, who came to be the largest grouping of the Shi'a, the doctrine of the *ghaiba* or "hiddenness" of the Twelfth Imam constituted a theme by which, one could say, religious limitations on war, particularly at the level of the *jus ad bellum*, became more stringent than among the Sunnis. Under optimum conditions, a divinely designated and guided Imam would lead the Muslims in the pursuit of justice and peace, including, insofar as necessary the use of lethal force against those resisting Islamic hegemony. In the absence of such an Imam, there was no authority for such a campaign. The notion that the label "legitimate war" could be applied only to wars conducted in defense of Islamic territory constituted a serious limit on the prerogative of political leaders to resort to war in situations of conflict.

Examples from Contemporary Islam

The Shiite emphasis on defensive war presents a good opportunity to move to more contemporary examples, not least because almost all important discussions of jihad over the last 150 years have stressed that it is a war in defense of Islamic values. This is so for Sunni and Shiite scholars alike, from the Indian Ahmad Khan (d. 1898) and the Egyptian Muhammad Abduh (d. 1905) to the late Shaykh al-Azhar Mahmud Shaltut and the Ayatullah Khumayni. Some contemporary writing on jihad is apologetic, intended to demonstrate to non-Muslims that Islam is a religion of peace. But much is a legitimate development of the basic ideas of the Qur'an and of classical Islamic thought. In particular, one finds again and again that religion—at least, Islamic religion—places restrictions on the kinds of wars one may fight and on the means by which victory may be pursued. The idea that wars should be fought for "secular" purposes—for example, the defense of a nation-state (as opposed to a state defined in Islamic terms)—is viewed with some suspicion, as opening the door to indiscriminate resort to and conduct of war. If one considers the case of the nine years' war between Iran and Iraq, there is some reason for this.

The war began when Iraq attacked Iran in September 1980. By most accounts, Iraq's leadership was concerned that propaganda efforts by the Islamic Republic of Iran would destabilize its population, which was probably 50 percent Twelver Shiite. In addition, there were long-standing border disputes for which agreements reached in 1975 provided only a partial solution. Worries about internal security, coupled with questions about the Islamic Republic's willingness to honor an agreement signed by the late Shah, moved Saddam Hussein to initiate a "sovereigns' war," in which a brief conflict would serve to demonstrate Iraqi resolve to Iran's revolutionary leadership. As the conflict escalated, this definition changed.[8] From Iraq's point of view, the war came to be a struggle (President Hussein referred to it as a jihad) to preserve the character of an Arab state against the "Persian enemy."

From the Iranian point of view, the war looked very different. The Ayatullah Khumayni, in particular, defined the war from the start in religious, that is to say Islamic, terms:

> You are fighting to protect Islam and he [Saddam Hussein] is fighting to destroy Islam. . . . There is absolutely no question of peace or compromise and we shall never have any discussions with them; because they are corrupt and perpetrators of corruption.[9]

> The damage caused by this criminal is irreparable unless he withdraws his forces, leaves Iraq and then abandons his corrupt government; he must leave the Iraqi people to decide their own fate. It is not a question of a fight between one government and another; it is a question of an invasion by an Iraqi non-Muslim Ba'thist against an Islamic country; and this is a rebellion by blasphemy against Islam.[10]

> Those who criticize us say: Why do you not compromise with these corrupt powers? It is because they see things through human eyes and analyse these things with a natural viewpoint. They do not know the views of God and how the prophets dealt with oppressors or else they know but pretend to be blind and deaf. To compromise with oppressors is to oppress. That is contrary to the views of all the prophets.[11]

From the Iranian point of view, it was precisely Iraq's "secularism," meaning its special blend of the symbols of pan-Arabism and the solidarity of Islamic and developing countries, which allowed Saddam Hussein and his colleagues to initiate a war against the Islamic Republic of Iran.[12] No *truly* religious or Islamic country would be so aggressive; such a war could never be construed as a "struggle in the path of God." On the other hand, Iran's leaders conceived their response as *defaᶜ*: a use of force "imposed" by Iraqi aggression. Iran fought to defend its borders—which were construed as the borders of an *Islamic* political entity. That such reasoning overlooked the problems posed by Iranian broadcasts of the Ayatullah Khumayni's speeches into Iraq, or the fears raised by calls for a "revolution without borders," goes without saying. One can overdraw the distinction between actual war and "war by other means." On the other hand, the Iranian response followed classical Shiite precedents. One is required to strive to command good and forbid evil by preaching and instruction, even in the absence of the Twelfth Imam. What one cannot do is pretend to initiate the jihad, in the sense of lethal force for the purposes of extending Islamic hegemony.

Still following the Iranian point of view, the distinction between nations fighting for religious and secular purposes was demonstrated by the conduct of the war. Iran's leadership thought of the conflict as a kind of "people's war," in which the entire nation would be engaged in a protracted struggle against an enemy whose military power exceeded its own. Such a war would require great sacrifice, even a readiness for martyrdom.

The Iranian version of a "people's war" would also require a reassessment of certain methods of conventional warfare, in favor of what the leadership called "Islamic warfare." For the most part, this seems to have meant that planning would proceed less along the lines of traditional concerns with strategic goals and their implementation and more along the lines of expressing Islamic motives.

The Ayatullah Khumayni spoke to this point when he said that the Iranians "think of Islam and wish to act according to Islamic teachings" in conducting their war with Iraq.[13] The Iranian military, in an attempt to implement this desire, set a policy against bombing cities.

Iran held to this policy into 1984, when the military did begin to engage in the bombing of cities like Basra. It must be noted, however, that the Iranian attacks on Iraqi cities generally followed Iraqi attacks that were far more devastating. Iran did not resort to chemical weapons, as did Iraq,[14] nor did it carry on a "tanker war" to the same extent as Iraq. Thus Iran's apparent shift in the midst of the war has something of the character of a *military* judgment. As Chubin and Tripp put it, "Iran's policy was to *respond* to Iraq's attacks at sea or on the cities to show that it was capable of doing so, and in order not to relinquish its right to do so or to acquiesce in Iraq's unilateral aims."[15]

By contrast, Iraq's war policy seems to have been dictated by a kind of cost-benefit analysis tied to its strategic aims. In the early phase of the war, when the conflict was defined by Saddam Hussein as a "sovereigns' war," the plan was for Iraqi forces to demonstrate their capacity to occupy territory. After the Iranians responded with their own use of force, Iraqi troops attacked the city of Khorramshahr, "reducing it largely to rubble in the process"—and then moved against Abadan.[16] The Iraqi president stated that these developments constituted a military defeat for Iran and should lead to Iran's recognition of Iraq's political and territorial rights.

Iran's military readiness, however, was greater than predicted, and the "sovereigns' war" quickly became a war of survival. Iraq's leadership determined that Iran must be taught according to the "logic of force," as the Minister of Foreign Affairs put it.[17] Such logic came to include attacks on the civilian population of Iran, the express aim being to cut support for the Khumayni regime.

> The rulers of Iran cannot go on with the war without the earnest backing, in word and deed, of their supporters. Therefore, the need to influence the relationship between the rulers of Iran and their supporters, by creating divergence between them on the question of war and peace, is of paramount importance.[18]

One aspect of Iraq's attempt to create such "divergence" focused on the use of chemical weapons against Iranian troops. Iraq's high command broadcast warnings that it had "modern weapons [which] will be used for the first time in war" and which had "not been used in previous attacks for humanitarian and ethical reasons. . . . If you execute the orders of Khomeini's regime . . . your death will be certain because this time we will use a weapon that will destroy any moving creature on the fronts."[19] Eventually, the United Nations issued a condemnation of Iraq for the use of such weapons, though Iraq officially denied the charge.

A second aspect of the strategy focused on attacks on Iranian cities. In 1984, these attacks provoked the Iranian bombardment of Basra and Baghdad, leading to an agreement to stop the "war of the cities." In 1985, 1986, and 1987, this agreement was repeatedly broken and restored, until a final series of attacks by Iraq culminated in Iran's acceptance of the cease-fire of 1988, a step Khumayni described as more bitter than poison.

More than anything else, such strategy bears witness to the definition that Iraq's leaders gave to the war. A "sovereigns' war" is limited in its objectives and its expenditure of the sovereign's military capacity. It need not be limited by considerations of discrimination, except as those serve the political interests of the sovereign. When those interests become identified with survival, as they did in the mind of Saddam Hussein, the calculus of military necessity can drive a nation to take extreme measures. By 1985, at the height of Iraq's policy of creating "divergence" between the Iranian people and their leaders, President Hussein spoke as follows:

> Iraq is now fighting only to prevent Iran from occupying Iraq. Technically speaking, the war may also end by one side achieving a military victory and occupying the land of the other. However, only the first alternative is realistic—one foiling the aim of the

other. When one side fails to achieve its goals through war, it
means defeat.[20]

According to Hussein, "Victory for us is to defend ourselves until the
other side gives up."[21] By that definition, Iran's acceptance of a cease-
fire in 1988 constituted victory for Iraq. The Gulf War forced the world
to deal with one part of the legacy of that "victory," as Saddam Hussein attempted once again to engage in a sovereigns' war—this time,
presenting himself as an *Islamic* sovereign, though still refusing to be
led by the norms of that tradition. The invasion of Kuwait, the bombing of cities, environmental warfare—all of these reflected Saddam
Hussein's perception of the special context that drove his policies, as
well as his sense of the threat posed by Allied force to the existence of
his regime.

Conclusion

We continue to live with the Gulf War and must deal with the
legacy of Saddam Hussein. We also live, and must come to grips with,
the continuing power of the idea that religion constitutes a, even *the*,
legitimate cause that justifies war. In the spring of 1989, I spoke at the
U.N. Church Center as part of a series of conferences dealing with Religion and Human Rights. The topic was Islam and Human Rights,
and Abdulaziz Sachedina also spoke. Professor Sachedina stressed the
positive role of Islam in the protection of basic rights, and drew a
question from one of those present: "What about the Armenian genocide? Didn't that happen under Islamic auspices?" I do not remember
Professor Sachedina's response, but I recall vividly a rejoinder made
by another member of the audience, a representative of the Iranian
delegation to the United Nations. "That was not Islam," he said. "That
was secularism."

So far as I am concerned, many aspects of the Armenian genocide, including the role of Islam, remain to be sorted out. But here I
am interested in the attitude exemplified by the Iranian representative's comment. For many devout Muslims, "secularism" indicates an
orientation that fails to respect religiously sanctioned norms, including those governing resort to and limitation of war. "Secular"
regimes, defined as they are in terms of the unity of a certain race,
class, or linguistic grouping, lack a universal moral sensibility. Their
will to power leads to the kind of aggressive and exploitative behavior exemplified by Iraq, first in its 1980 attack against Iran, now in its
annexation of Kuwait. In the end, those who deny the necessity of divine guidance come to behave in ways that are not only irreligious

but inhumane—that is the message of the Iranian representative's comment, and, depending on how one reads the evidence, it can also be the meaning of Iraq's behavior during the long war with Iran.

On the other hand, Islam serves to limit the occasion and conduct of war in very explicit ways. Classical and contemporary Muslim theorists propose that the only legitimate wars are those "in the path of God," indicating wars fought with the aim either of extending Islamic hegemony, thus improving the chances for human beings to live together in peace and justice, or of defending an established Islamic polity against the kind of aggression that might interfere with its capacity to be ruled by Islamically sanctioned norms. The religious aims of such wars also establish limits on means, in which a notion of discrimination plays an important part. This notion is not the same as the just war distinction between combatants and noncombatants, as will be seen in chapter 4. It is, however, an attempt to distinguish the innocent from the guilty on the enemy side and thus to indicate the limits of acceptable behavior in war. If Iraq's behavior in the war with Iran may be read as indicative of the way a certain kind of "secularism" affects resort to and limitation of war, then I suppose Iran's behavior indicates the way that religion can serve as a limitation on war.[22]

For my part, I am not particularly interested in drawing such general lessons from this or any other case of thinking about war. What interests me is, first, that *some people* draw these kinds of lessons and, second, the ways in which that fact serves to reinforce elements of Islamic tradition that focus on religion as a *casus belli*. Concurrently, it interests me that the Islamic case seems to further the critique offered by various scholars of the Bainton thesis that notions of religion as a cause of war lend themselves to a crusade mentality, where considerations of discrimination and proportionality pale in the light of a holy cause.

What are students of the ethics of war to do in the light of these considerations? Most of us have learned from Victoria that "difference in religion is not a just cause of war"; if we have not learned that from Victoria, we have learned it as a principle of international law. That principle, coupled with the influence of Bainton's thesis, leads many to suspect that Muslim conceptions of war will lead us into a new version of the age of religious wars, in which Christians and Muslims, or, better, Western and Islamic cultures, will meet in a never-ending series of conflicts. It seems to me that this argument is not very carefully drawn: the Islamic tradition does not say that difference in religion, in and of itself, is a *casus belli*. Rather, it indicates that, where religion is a significant factor in defining political identity, the ways people talk about resort to and limitation of war will frequently involve religious terminology. For a just war theorist, the problem is to get beyond the received notions concerning "holy war" in order seriously to engage the Islamic tradition and its ways of thinking about resort to and limitation of war. One way to do this would involve sustained exploration of the various appeals to "religion" in the Islamic tradition. One might ask, When Muslims talk about religion in war, do they always mean the same things we do? Or are some appeals to "religion" really appeals to what a just war theorist would classify as moral or political causes for war? For example, when Muslims speak of defending Islamic territory, what do they mean but the defense of territorial integrity? Or when the Qur'an speaks of the "Sanction given unto those who fight because they have been wronged. . . . Those who have been driven from their homes unjustly only because they said: Our Lord is Allah" (22:39–40), what does it mean but the defense of human rights? The problem with this approach is that one is speaking about a defense of the territorial integrity of a political entity characterized by its acceptance of *Islamic* norms; or, in the case of Qur'an 22:39–40, one is dealing with a justification for war that refers to the importance of protecting *religious* values ("For had it not been for Allah's repelling some men by means of others, cloisters and churches and oratories and mosques, wherein the name of Allah is oft mentioned, would assuredly have been pulled down"). The analogy between just war tradition and Islamic thought about war is made complex by the way that moral concepts are connected with religion in the Islamic case. As Abdulaziz Sachedina has recently put it, some aspects of the Islamic tradition approach the question of war by reference to religiously sanctioned moral norms.[23] Both qualifiers are important: "religiously sanctioned" and "moral." The latter suggests a point of connection between just war tradition and Islamic thought. The former suggests difference, at least with respect to contemporary manifestations of just war tradition.

One way to think about the point of comparative studies of ethics and war is to consider their potential for revising the traditions of particular cultures (like the West and Islam) in ways that would yield a new, universal tradition on the restraint of war. I have some sympathy with that idea. But the path to that goal includes a number of smaller projects. From my perspective, the more immediate point of discussions of Islamic conceptions of war is less the development of a new, more inclusive just war tradition than it is the increase of understanding of the variety of ways human beings can think about the justification and conduct of war. In this perspective, the term "just war tradition" signifies one culture's ongoing conversation about the moral issues raised by the political use of lethal force. For a variety of reasons, not the least of which is simply learning, it is important now to enlarge the scope of that conversation by attending to Islam and to other religious and cultural traditions that heretofore have not been a decisive part of that conversation. It may be that this enlargement, coupled with the increased presence of Muslims in the academy and in European and American culture as a whole, will lead to a new, more inclusive just war tradition. More immediately, I hope attention to Islamic perspectives on the use of lethal force will contribute to the development of wisdom among the architects of American foreign policy. But it is also worthwhile, if less grand, simply to attend to examples of Islamic conceptions of war and thereby be reminded of the import of Weber's comment: "Neither religion nor men are open books. . . . In religious matters 'consistency' has been the exception and not the rule." There is something attractive, even comforting, about the notion that religion as a *casus belli* leads inevitably to total war. It suggests that, if we just keep religion out of war, we can safeguard humanitarian aims. But history—humanity—is not so simple. The way to a practical universality of the just war tradition must be through many layers of historical, or even human, thickness. We cannot, even in the service of notions of psychological or logical consistency, avoid the variety present in the historical (actual) relationship of religion and war.

CHAPTER FOUR

Islam and the Conduct of War: The Question of *Jus in Bello* Restraints

There can be no question that the distinction between combatants and noncombatants, and the subsequent "immunity from harm" of the latter, is central to Western notions of the limitation of war. The developed form of the just war tradition stresses this distinction as a part of its concern for justice in war (the *jus in bello*).

Why this is so is a matter of some dispute. Some give a philosophical explanation. According to Robert Phillips, for example, the distinction rests on the "categorical prohibition of murder."[1] At bottom, then, combatants and noncombatants are distinguished for moral reasons.

Others provide a theological explanation for the distinction. Paul Ramsey, for example, argued that the idea of noncombatant immunity originated in the attempt of Christians to be faithful to the command "Love your neighbor as yourself" in the realm of politics. Love justified killing in war, as a way to protect the innocent from aggression. But the

> justification of participation in conflict at the same time severely limited war's conduct. What justified also limited! Since it was for the sake of the innocent and helpless of earth that the Christian first thought himself obliged to make war against an enemy whose objective deeds had to be stopped, since only for their sakes does a Christian justify himself in resisting by any means even an enemy-neighbor, he could never proceed to kill equally innocent people as a means of getting at the enemy's forces. . . . The same considerations which justify killing the bearer of hostile

force by the same stroke prohibit non-combatants from ever being directly attacked with deliberate intent.[2]

There is a sense in which such arguments are convincing. If one is interested in why it is that just war tradition worries about distin-guishing between legitimate and illegitimate targets in the first place; in other words, if one wants to understand how it is that (at least some) persons come to think it important to practice some degree of discrimination in attacking enemy targets in war—then Phillips, Ram-sey, or others may suffice. But one has to go some distance from the "categorical prohibition of murder" or the attempt to be faithful to the love command in the realm of politics to get to a list like the following, set forth by a Roman Catholic theologian in a discussion of the ethics of bombing enemy cities during World War II:

> Farmers, fishermen, foresters, lumberjacks, dressmakers, milliners, bakers, printers, textile workers, millers, painters, paper hangers, piano tuners, plasterers, shoemakers, cobblers, tailors, upholsterers, furniture makers, cigar and cigarette makers, glove makers, hat makers, suit makers, food processors, dairymen . . . [the list goes on].

All these, says the author, are in the category of noncombatants, and it is therefore impermissible to make them the direct target of a military attack.[3] Granted that moral principles and the ethics of the Gospel have their place in the development of just war thinking, how is it that the tradition came to such specific judgments about targets that are "off limits," never to be the object of direct military action?

This chapter begins with the suggestion that the connections be-tween noncombatant immunity and moral principles or theological be-liefs are not so clear as some would have us believe. The notion of noncombatancy is one way—the way most characteristic of just war tradition—of discriminating between the innocent and the guilty in war. It is a socially constructed way of specifying who the innocent are.

This suggestion is not particularly new. In a number of his works, James Turner Johnson has made the point that the just war emphasis on noncombatancy grew out of at least two distinctive sources: on the one hand, the canon law tradition of the church, which stressed that persons who do not make war (priests, monks, merchants, and others) should not have war made against them; on the other, the chivalric code of medieval knights, in which those having military prowess agree not to exercise their power against others weaker than them-selves (women, children, the aged and infirm). Writing in particular about Ramsey's argument, Johnson indicates that it obscures "the centuries of struggle to limit the ill effects of war by protecting noncombatants from harm."[4] Noncombatant immunity may begin with concerns about the "categorical prohibition of murder" or the love command. But such concerns only become specific following a long and arduous process involving the interests of religious, political, legal, and military institutions.

These considerations are important when one examines the Islamic tradition on the conduct of war. In most instances, that tradition does not contain a notion of noncombatant immunity, purely and simply. That does not mean that Islamic thought is inattentive to the concern for justice in war, however. Rather, it indicates that the substance of "justice" and "innocence" takes on a distinctive cast in Islamic thought. The Islamic tradition on *jus in bello* restraints, like its Western counterpart, reflects a cultural consensus on the conduct of war: a consensus that owes much to moral principles and theological concerns but is also indebted to political and military factors.

Classical Islam and the Rules of War

We have already seen that classical Islamic perspectives on the rules of war make use of a number of sources. Some of these are self-evident in the writings of the Sunni scholars. For example, the treatise of Muhammad ibn al-Hasan al-Shaybani (d. 804 or 805) called *Kitab al-Siyar* ("the book of conduct," especially conduct of international relations), appeals to a number of *hadith* related to the conduct of war. One of the most famous of these relates Muhammad's challenge to his troops to "do good. . . . Fight in the name of God and in the 'path of God.'. . . Combat [only] those who disbelieve in God."[5] Muhammad goes on to forbid treachery and mutilation and, most important in connection with our interests, orders his forces not to kill children. Other sayings attributed to the Prophet reinforce and add to this one, thus creating a kind of list of persons with immunity. Al-Shaybani cites the following:

> He [of the enemy] who has reached puberty should be killed, but he who has not should be spared.
>
> The Apostle of God prohibited the killing of women.
>
> The Apostle of God said: "You may kill the adults of the unbelievers, but spare their minors—the youth."
>
> Whenever the Apostle of God sent forth a detachment he said to

it: "Do not cheat or commit treachery, nor should you mutilate or kill children, women, or old men."[6]

As presented by al-Shaybani, these reports of the Prophet's example form the foundation for Islamic reasoning about certain issues in the conduct of war. This is consonant with the general approach of classical Sunni thought, which was still in a developmental phase when al-Shaybani wrote. The phenomenon of devotion to the Prophet Muhammad, and the sense that all Muslim behavior should be systematically, consistently scrutinized in terms of the guidance of God, must be seen as a primary motivation for the development of classical Sunni thinking on war (and on other matters).

Sunni conceptions of the rules of war do not rest entirely on the example of the Prophet, however. As indicated elsewhere, the Sunni theorists developed and presupposed a particular interpretation of the Qur'an, which may be read, at least in part, as an apologia for the conquests of the mid to late seventh century. A scholar such as al-Shaybani thus presupposed the connection of Islam with an imperial state and its power—specifically, the power of the Abbasid caliphate, by whom he (as others) was appointed as chief *qadi* or religious judge. It was the task of scholars like al-Shaybani to make judgments concerning the religious legitimacy of the Abbasid caliph's policies; most (though not all) of the time, he was able to identify those policies as in the interests of Islam.

Finally, religious scholars such as al-Shaybani developed their ideas about the conduct of war in connection with military practice. Fred Donner has suggested that a number of practices, including notions of who may or may not be killed in war, were adopted into Islam from the pre-Islamic culture of Arabia or from the conquered regions.[7] I presume this is true, though the present state of our knowledge is short on details. What is clear from the works of a scholar like al-Shaybani is that Muslims who thought about the conduct of war were familiar with the basics of military practice and strategy as these existed during the period of imperial Islam. The Sunni *fuqaha*, or religious scholars, did not, then, develop their ideas about war in a vacuum. Their work presupposed and contributed to the development of a cultural consensus on the conduct of war: a consensus in which religious, moral, political, and military factors would all have a part to play. These points become more clear if one considers their answers to several basic questions: *Who* must fight? *When*? Against *whom*? *How* may the enemy be dealt with? *Where* does one find the enemy? and, By what *means* may military success be pursued?

To begin: *Who* must fight? To a certain extent, the answer depends on what type of war one envisions. For al-Shaybani, as for other

Sunni intellectuals, a "normal" war is connected with the effort to extend the boundaries of Islamic territory. This struggle, for which the preferred means is the spread of the Islamic message through preaching, teaching, and the like, may nevertheless take on the character of war. When it does, there is a collective obligation (in Arabic, *fard kifaya*) laid upon the Muslim community to supply the necessary manpower for a successful military action. Adult males who are ablebodied and have no debts are obligated to do their part for the sake of Islam—though this does not mean that all such males are obliged to fight. It is permissible, even exemplary, for some to sponsor others. So long as there is a full complement of men to fight, it is legitimate for some to take the role of sponsor, providing weapons, horses, and the like for those who will actually fight.[8]

If the situation changes, however, so that the aim becomes the *defense* of Islamic territory against enemy attacks, the nature of the obligation shifts. It is no longer *fard kifaya*, but *fard ayn*, an "individual obligation," in which each person must do all that he (or she) can for the sake of Islam. While the focus of the obligation (adult, ablebodied males) remains the same, the distinction between "collective" and "individual" responsibilities is intended to reflect increased urgency.

When one fights is already suggested by the preceding paragraphs. We must recall the Sunni scholars' division of the world into *dar al-islam*, the territory where Islamic norms had official recognition, and *dar al-harb*, the territory where the willful human tendency toward heedlessness (*jahiliyya*) and ignorance of God prevailed. The latter was, by definition, the sphere of war, disorder, and injustice. Even when these factors were mitigated, as in the case of a Christian empire or state, there was the danger of misguidance. And thus the territory of Islam—really, the world—could not be a secure place until and unless Islamic hegemony was acknowledged everywhere. To secure such hegemony was the goal of the jihad, or "struggle in the path of God." According to the Sunni theorists, war or jihad by means of killing is justified when a people resists or otherwise stands in opposition to the legitimate goals of Islam.

In the "normal" circumstance, such resistance is indicated by a refusal to acknowledge Islamic hegemony. Following the example of the Prophet, Muslims are to invite their enemies either to become Muslims or to submit to Islamic hegemony by paying tribute. Acceptance of the invitation indicates a willingness to live under the norms of Islam. But if neither invitation is accepted, the state of war becomes actual.

Thus, in answer to the question, *Against whom* (is war fought)? one must say, The people who refuse to submit; the people living in the territory of war, individually and collectively. They have refused to acknowledge Islam and so become the "people of war" *(ahl al-harb)*. The sole exception would be those who reside in the territory of war but are themselves Muslims—say, merchants traveling among the "people of war." As I shall show, these are not considered legitimate targets for direct attack by the Muslims, though their deaths may be brought about indirectly.

These comments suggest a kind of collective responsibility for refusal of Islamic hegemony. In a sense, each member of the resistant people becomes an enemy of Islam. At the same time, however, the Prophetic reports cited above indicate that children, women, and others are exempt from killing in war. How, in light of the collective guilt of the "people of war," are these exemptions to be understood? Some scholars (e.g., al-Shafii, d. 820 C.E.) indicated that the Muslims were to make distinctions between residents of the territory of war who are polytheists and those who are not. The Prophet's statement prohibiting the killing of women, for example, was to be interpreted as applying only to Jews and Christians.[9] Even with this interpretation, however, the problem remains complicated: Even those whom everyone agreed should be exempt from killing (children) could be legitimate targets for other types of force—for example, enslavement. And all enemy persons may, under certain conditions, be regarded as booty for the Muslim forces.

A distinction suggested by Ibn Rushd (Averroes) is useful in this connection.[10] Ibn Rushd notes that there are three ways in which an enemy may be "damaged": He (or she) is able to suffer harm in terms of property, person (i.e., life and limb), and liberty. Taking the second category first, one notes that all those among the enemy who actually engage the Muslims in battle (i.e., soldiers) are legitimate objects of force. If these are killed, there is no difficulty. Indeed, Ibn Rushd says that even soldiers taken as prisoners of war may be killed according to the discretion of the commander of the Muslims. The commander has two options: If the decision is against killing the soldier/POWs, they must be taken as booty; the commander decides which course to take after calculation of the costs and benefits (i.e., to the Muslims) of each. The only exceptions to this rule occur if soldiers who have been taken as POWs become Muslims—in which case their *person* is inviolable, although their *liberty* is not, and they are to be regarded as booty—or if the enemy soldiers can show they were taken under false pretenses— for example, they were in possession of a valid pledge of security from the Muslims at the time of their capture.[11]

According to Ibn Rushd, women and children are in a somewhat different category. In one sense, they, along with land, stock, and other goods, are "property." They belong to the (male) soldiers who actually fight in the cause of the enemy. Any "damage" suffered by them is thus a harm or a type of damage done to male warriors. Yet the rules intended to govern Muslim behavior restrict the Muslims' military options where women and children are involved—a fact that is not altogether consistent with the idea that they belong to the enemy soldiers.

The first and most rigorous of these applies to children, who are not to be killed. This is based on a Prophetic injunction (cited above). Children, in other words, are not to suffer damage to life or limb.

Is this a notion of noncombatant immunity? Prima facie, the effect is that intended by the just war tradition: a class of persons is set apart as protected or immune from direct military attack. Two special features of the Muslim protection must be noted, however. First, insofar as children are not to be *killed*, some of the evidence suggests the reason is that they have not reached the age of refusal of Islam.[12] They are in the custody of their parents and as nonbelievers are subject to "damage." But their responsibility is diminished by their age (and competence). They are not therefore subject to *lethal* damage.

Second, the prescription against killing children is only given full force in the case of children taken captive. One can easily imagine situations in which children might become victims of the sword during a military action. The just war tradition, with its notions of noncombatant immunity, could nevertheless consider such actions under the notion of double effect. The deaths of children would thus be described as "accidental"; the killing is unintentional or, better, coincidental to the main object of battle.[13]

Sunni scholars undertake such reasoning only in the case of Muslim children, however. Thus, in a case where a city is besieged, or a ship attacked by archers, and it is known that Muslims will be killed, the notion of unavoidable yet unintentional killing appears.[14] But in the case of non-Muslim children, the Muslim forces are not responsible. "They are from them," said the Prophet upon hearing that some women and children had been killed by Muslims during a night raid.[15] That is, the deaths are not the fault of Muslims. Responsibility devolves to those who, in their decision-making capacity, have chosen to resist Islam. The need to make excuses or offer justifications for unintended killings, so much a part of the phenomenon of double-effect reasoning, does not seem to be present.

We may interpret the rulings of some theorists with respect to women along the same lines. I have mentioned already that some could argue that, in the case of polytheists, women should be killed. I should note here that such theorists only really debate the issue when they discuss cases of women taken as prisoners of war. While battle is raging, they simply assume that enemy women may be killed. Others take a different line. For example, al-Shaybani argued that women *cap-tives* are to be taken as booty (in other words, must not be killed), even at cost to the Muslims. Thus, in a discussion of the difficulties that may emerge in the transport of human booty, al-Shaybani argues as fol-lows. If the leader of the Muslims has no means of transporting this booty, he should kill the males. But women and children must be spared; the Muslims should find a way to acquire means of transport-ing them to the territory of Islam. Why are women spared, and men not? There is the word of the Prophet, of course, and that is actually all the reason al-Shaybani gives. Prima facie, this looks like a notion of noncombatant immunity. But one must note: al-Shaybani assumes the "controlled" situation of captivity. In this context, women are not sub-ject to damage that deprives them of life, while their husbands, fa-thers, and brothers are. Whether this distinction is based on an estimate of "probable threat" (the males might become a kind of "fifth column" in the "territory of Islam") or on a notion that women, like children, do not bear as much responsibility for the enemy's resis-tance to Islam is an open question.[16] In either case, the distinction be-tween male and female prisoners need not indicate a notion of noncombatant immunity, *as such.*

Where one deals with the enemy is connected with judgments about *how* one may deal with him or her. We have already seen that there is a difference between the treatment of enemy persons "on the battlefield" and "in the camp." Similarly, the status of enemy persons varies, as do the duties/rights of Muslim combatants in relation to them, according to whether they are located in the territory of war or of Islam. In his discussion of booty, for example, al-Shaybani indicates that, while every free Muslim male who participates in the jihad has a right to a share of the spoil, such rights are not to be exercised until the spoil has been returned to the *dar al-Islam* ("the place of [Islamic] secu-rity"). One reason for this is practical—all participants deserve a share, so it is best to wait until the campaign is over to make divisions.[17]

A second reason has to do with status, however. In a discussion of a married woman captive, al-Shaybani indicates that, so long as she and her husband remain together (i.e., in terms of territory), their marriage holds and no Muslim has rights to her. That is, unless one of the partners is taken to the territory of Islam before the other. Then, "the wedlock would be broken."[18] In a similar vein, booty pledged as "prime" (i.e., excepted from the general booty and belonging to who-ever captures it) cannot be used or sold until it is taken to the territory of Islam.[19]

As to the *means* of war, Sunni jurists seem in general to have held the principle *vim vi repellere licit* (approximately, "it is allowed to repel force with equal force"). Thus, al-Shaybani:

> [An inquirer asked:] Do you think that it is objectionable for the believers to destroy whatever towns of the territory of war that they may encounter?

> [Al-Shaybani answered:] No. Rather do I hold that this would be commendable. For do you not think that it is in accordance with God's saying, in His Book: "Whatever palm trees you have cut down or left standing upon their roots, has been by God's permission, in order that the ungodly ones might be humiliated." So, I am in favor of whatever they did to deceive and anger the enemy.[20]

In another place, al-Shaybani discusses various modes of attack. The context is siege warfare, and al-Shaybani approves of the use of arrows, lances, flooding, burning with fire, and mangonels. This is so, even though the issue is specifically framed to indicate the presence of "slaves, women, old men, and children" in the city. Further, "even if they had among them [Muslims], there would be no harm to do all of that to them." Why?

> If the Muslims stopped attacking the inhabitants of the territory of war for any of the reasons that you have stated, they would be unable to go to war at all, for there is no city in the territory of war in which there is no one at all of these you have mentioned.[21]

Are there any exceptions to this general rule? Yes, but these again point to a difference between the Western, just war tradition and the reasoning of Sunni theorists with respect to the rules of war. The first exception has to do, for example, with the killing of children. It is not just any children who are at risk, however; the problem for the Sunni theorists emerges because the case in question has to do with *Muslim* children. These are at risk in a case where military concerns are paramount. We are to imagine a case in which the residents of a besieged city shield themselves with Muslim children. According to al-Shaybani, "the warriors should aim at the inhabitants of the territory of war and not the Muslim children."[22] Here, unlike the reasoning employed in the case of non-Muslim children killed during a military action (discussed above), we see Islamic thinkers presenting a clear parallel to the just war notion of double effect, in which the killing of some is justified or excused as the unintended or unwanted side effect of a legitimate military action.

The other exception to al-Shaybani's general rule has to do with
the "pledge of security" (aman) by which a citizen of the territory of
war comes under the protection of a Muslim. Under certain conditions, this provides a temporary immunity from attack.[23]

What shall we make of the judgments described thus far? It does
not seem to me that the Sunni theorists actually articulate a notion of
noncombatant immunity, as just war thinkers understand it. If we
consider, however, that the larger category of just war reasoning is actually "discrimination" and that noncombatant immunity is a socially
constructed way of implementing the concern to distinguish the innocent from the guilty, this discrepancy is not alarming. As previously
mentioned, contemporary work on the genesis of noncombatant immunity suggests that this just war notion is the result of a consensus
reached through the interaction of a variety of elements: religious,
moral, military, and political. The same suggestion applies to the
thought of classical Sunni theorists.

We might say it this way: Islam recognizes, even as other religious and moral traditions, that there is a "categorical prohibition of
murder." Muslims recognize that there are moral obligations that apply to human beings, even in time of war.

But prohibitions of murder, or applications of moral obligations
in the context of war, need specification. If murder is "unjust killing" or
the "direct taking of innocent life," one must know how to identify injustice or innocence. Formal categories are insufficient. We must know
what the material content of such notions are, if they are to be mean-
ingful for an exercise such as the attempt to limit war. With respect to
concerns to discriminate between the innocent and the guilty in war,
Western culture accomplished the work of specification in terms of the
distinction between combatants and noncombatants—deciding, in a
sense, to assign innocence or guilt according to the roles people play.
For just war tradition, "soldiers," qua soldiers, are not innocent—regardless of their subjective involvement with the war effort. "Civilians," qua civilians, are innocent—again, with little or no attention to
the fact that they may be leading the cheers in favor of the war.[24]

Classical Sunni theorists dealt with this question in a different
way. For them, guilt and innocence had to do with religious and political factors. How does one fit in the scheme of things, as understood
from the Muslim point of view? Specifically, is one a part of a people
who are in opposition to the establishment of an order of justice and
peace (i.e., an Islamic order), or not? And what is one's place in that
people? If one is a leader (an adult, ablebodied male), one's guilt is obvious. If one is a follower (child, woman), one's guilt may be diminished. In either case, one is liable to "damage"; the question is only

what type, and how. And, given the goals of Islamic hegemony, the *means* of war that are appropriate are affected. Military might is meant to serve the cause of justice. It should not be used indiscriminately, if one means by that "carelessly." Considerations of proportionality are important, since one wants to shed no more blood than is necessary. But the necessities of the war effort motivated by religious considerations allow for considerable discretion. If women and children are killed in the pursuit of battle, it is not the fault of the Muslims. "They are from them." The leaders of the people of war are at fault for the death of their "innocents."

Rules of War in the Case of Rebellion[25]

This fact—that is, the determination of discrimination by religious, political, and military factors—is further illustrated by al-Shaybani's discussion of the rules for fighting against dissenters and rebels.

Al-Shaybani's discussion of these rules begins with the citation of a report concerning the practice of Ali b. Abi Talib (fourth leader of the Muslims after the Prophet; d. 661 C.E.). Ali's precedent is especially important in this regard, since his caliphate began with and eventually was ended by the action of dissenters. According to al-Shaybani's report, Ali "said in the Battle of the Camel: 'Whoever flees [from us] shall not be chased, no [Muslim] prisoner of war shall be killed, no wounded in battle shall be dispatched, no enslavement [of women and children] shall be allowed, and no property [of a Muslim] shall be confiscated.' "[26] This precedent forms the basis for the following exchange:

> If there were two parties of believers, one of them is rebellious . . . and the other loyal . . ., and the former was defeated by the latter, would not the loyal party have the right to chase the fugitives [of the other party], kill their prisoners, and dispatch the wounded?

> He [al-Shaybani] replied: No, it should never be allowed to do so if none of the rebels has survived and no group remained with whom refuge might be taken; but if a group of them has survived with whom refuge might be taken, then their prisoners could be killed, their fugitives pursued, and their wounded dispatched.[27]

Several aspects of this exchange are of interest. In particular, note the difference in treatment of the rebels (who are Muslims) from that of the people of war. Even according to al-Shaybani's judgment, which seems less generous than that of Ali b. Abi Talib, there is a clear distinction: after the rebellion is over, no prisoners are to be killed. Why is this

the case? Because, even though the rebels are a threat to order in the
territory of Islam, they remain Muslims. If rebels are killed in a war
they have provoked, such killing is right. But there remains a certain
obligation to them that is distinct from that owed to the people of war.
Thus, the "loyalists" cannot impose a peace that requires the rebels to
pay tribute. This is so, says al-Shaybani, "because [the rebels] are Muslims; therefore, nothing should be taken from their property, for this
would amount to kharaj" (i.e., "land tax," in effect, tribute).[28] Again, if
a group of *dhimmiyya* (Jews and Christians who have agreed to pay
tribute in recognition of Muslim hegemony) join with the rebels in
fighting, the fact that the rebels remain Muslims protects the *dhimmiyya*.

> If the rebels sought the assistance of a group of Dhimmis, who
> took part in the fighting along with them, do you think that [the
> Dhimmis' participation in the fighting] would be regarded as a
> violation of their agreement [with the Muslims]?
>
> [Al-Shaybani replied]: No.
>
> I asked: Why?
>
> He replied: Because they were in the company of a group of Mus-
> lims.[29]

In the case of Muslim rebels, the cause of war is different than in
the war against the people of war. And thus the notion of discrimination is applied somewhat differently. Guilt is established, not by a refusal to acknowledge the priority of Islam, but by an uprising against
the established authority in the territory of Islam. After the war is over,
the idea seems to be that the rebels are restored to the house of Islam.
· During the conduct of fighting, however, al-Shaybani remains a
proponent of *vim vi repellere licit*. One notes the following exchange
(which is nearly an exact parallel to his judgment concerning appropriate means in an action against the people of war):

> I asked: Would it be objectionable to you if the loyalists shot [the
> rebels] with arrows, inundated [their positions] with water, at-
> tacked them with manjaniqs (mangonels), and burned them with
> fire?
>
> He replied: No harm in doing anything of this sort.
>
> I asked: Would a sudden attack at night be objectionable to you?
>
> He replied: No harm in it.[30]

In other passages, al-Shaybani takes up questions involving women who fight with the rebels; he says that they may be killed.[31] If such women are taken prisoner, however, they are not to be executed but imprisoned until the fighting ends.[32] In that sense they are treated as a nonfighting (male) slave would be. Should a slave or freeman be fighting with the rebels, however, he would be executed, so long as the fighting continues.[33]

The rules governing the fighting of rebels thus continue to demonstrate the qualification of moral concerns for discrimination in war by religious, political, and military considerations. The development of discrimination in classical, Sunni thought is not fully consistent with the specification of the developed just war tradition with its distinction between combatants and noncombatants. But it is not altogether inconsistent, either.

The Jus in Bello in Contemporary Islam

When one turns from these classical materials to more contemporary discussions, one is first struck by the scarcity of *jus in bello* materials. Unlike the classical theorists, contemporary Muslim thinkers seem mostly interested in the *jus ad bellum*. There are a number of possible explanations for this fact. Most convincing, prima facie, is an explanation that refers to the recent history of Islam. When, in 1924, the "Young Turks" abolished the Ottoman Caliphate, they did away with one of the most important institutions of classical Islam. The Caliphate had really ceased long before that date to function as classical theory demanded. Nevertheless it provided a symbol of the continuity of Islamic civilization through the centuries. The Turkish abolition of the institution signified the decision of an elite to institute radical reform: in effect, to depart from the classical patterns of Islamic culture and to develop new ways of ordering life. The Turks led the way in "secularization"; they, and those who followed their example, began to look to sources other than those utilized by the Sunni theorists to discuss affairs of state. Indeed, for most of this century the planning of military and political strategy for Muslim countries and movements has been in the hands of elites who have drawn heavily on traditions that are not specifically Islamic. To put it another way, Muslims who have been doing the most thinking about the conduct of war have not been doing so as self-conscious developers of the tradition of Islamic thought.

The Palestine Liberation Organization (PLO) provides a prime example of such developments. Until recently, many of the official documents that set forth the justification and strategy for the "armed struggle" against Israel spoke the language of Arab nationalism and drew less on Islamic traditions than on models of revolutionary struggle or "people's war" developed by the Vietnamese or the Algerians in their struggles against colonialism.[34]

According to the Palestine National Assembly meeting in Cairo in July 1978, the enemy consists of "three interdependent forces": Israel, Zionism, and world imperialism, of which the United States is the chief director.[35] Israel is "the tool of the Zionist movement and a human and geographical base for world Imperialism. It is a concentration and jumping-off point for Imperialism in the heart of the Arab homeland, to strike at the hopes of the Arab nation for liberation, unity, and progress."[36]

To struggle against this enemy, by whatever means one can muster, is just. Correspondingly, those who support the enemy or who stand idly by incur guilt and become, in some sense, legitimate targets of military force. Ideological considerations become the measure of the notion of discrimination.[37]

That this is so is further indicated by statements of PLO leaders that *do* indicate some considerations in accord with discrimination. For example, in his November 1974 speech to the United Nations, Yassir Arafat declared:

> Since its inception, our revolution has not been motivated by racial or religious factors. Its target has never been the Jew, as a person, but racist Zionism and aggression. In this sense, ours is also a revolution for the Jew, as a human being. We are struggling so that Jews, Christians, and Muslims may live in equality, enjoying the same rights and assuming the same duties, free from racial or religious discrimination. . . . *We distinguish between Judaism and Zionism.* While we maintain our opposition to the colonialist Zionist movement, we respect the Jewish faith.[38]

The PLO's war with Israel, here as elsewhere, is defined in ideological, even territorial, terms. The just or innocent are those who do not join in supporting Zionism in its "usurpation" of Palestinian land (and its denial of Palestinian rights). The unjust, correspondingly, are those who are active in support of Zionism, including citizens of imperialist powers who do not distance themselves from their nation's policy. According to the 1968 National Assembly, the method of armed resistance best suited to the interests of the Palestinians is a protracted war which will expose Zionism and "its complicity with world imperialism" and will "point out the damage and complications [Zionism] causes to the interests and security of many countries, and the threat it constitutes to world peace."[39]

What one might like (even, from classical Islamic tradition, expect) to see is a greater attention to the question of degrees of guilt on the part of the citizens of Israel and the "imperialist" powers. Should children, for example, be counted as guilty? The closest that one comes to such attention is the willingness of Palestinian spokespersons to forswear military actions outside the territory of Palestine. There is a recognition here of the difficulties of "guilt by association," and a specification that the conflict is really about usurpation of territory. Correspondingly, the Palestinian leadership's unwillingness to forswear military operations inside the borders of Israel points once again to the criterion by which guilt is established: those who indicate support for Zionism by dwelling in the territory of Palestine become legitimate targets for military action. And as to children, one sometimes hears Palestinians argue that Israeli children are "placed" in the land by supporters of Zionism. In a manner reminiscent of the example of the Prophet Muhammad, Palestinian activists thus argue that such children become targets, not through their own doing, but through the action of others. Their deaths are unfortunate but do not indicate Palestinian guilt. Rather, the guilt is upon those who placed the children in the land.[40]

In more explicitly Islamic materials, two types of writing have been predominant in modern discussions of jihad: one is apologetic and seeks to indicate to the world that Islam is not a "religion of the sword." The other is revolutionary and seeks to indicate the justice of Islamic struggle against imperialism. In either case, one finds only the most tenuous discussion of the conduct of war; the obvious reason being that one is not dealing with treatises written by people like al-Shaybani, who were, at least at times, actually engaged in questions of policy.

For an example of apologetic literature, I turn to Mahmud Shaltut's *The Koran and Fighting*, which received brief mention in chapter 2 of this volume.[41] Shaltut's treatise illustrates the thought of one of the leading spokesmen for "establishment Islam" in Egypt during this century. His purpose in writing is to illumine the relation between Islam and warfare, a topic that he says

> is of practical importance in our times, as wars are being fought all over the world, engaging everybody's attention. Moreover, it has a theoretical significance, as many adherents of other religions constantly take up this subject with a view to discredit Islam. Therefore, people would do well to learn the Koranic rules with regard to fighting, its causes and its ends, and so come to recognize the wisdom of the Koran in this respect: its desire for

peace and its aversion against bloodshed and killing for the sake
of the vanities of the world and out of sheer greediness and
lust.[42]

According to Shaltut, the mission of Muhammad, expressed in
the Qur'an, is as "a bringer of good tidings and as a warner."[43] The
Qur'an summons humanity to submit to God; this is "natural" to humanity, though it is difficult for those "who do not reflect." True submission is a matter of the heart; it cannot be forced. Thus the Qur'anic
dictum: "No compulsion in religion" (2:256). Therefore, fighting cannot be a part of the Islamic mission.

The Qur'an does of course contain verses on fighting, which Shaltut must now explain. He does so by arguing that these verses deal
with the defense of the Islamic community. "Permission is granted to
those who are fought because they have suffered wrong; verily to help
them Allah is able. Who have been expelled from their dwellings without justification, except that they say: 'Our Lord is Allah'" (22:39–41).
All justified war is defensive, according to Shaltut. There is no hint in
the Qur'an of a justification of "conversion by force."

Thus far, Shaltut has dealt with the *jus ad bellum*. But what of the
jus in bello? Here we find much less. According to Shaltut, the Qur'an
strengthens the morale of the nation for fighting. It deals, in other
words, with "factors that may lead to cowardice and weakness" and
encourages self-sacrifice for the defense of the Islamic community.[44]
Further, the Qur'an gives advice on the preparation of the material
power necessary to war. God has said: "We formerly sent Our messengers with the Evidences, and We sent down with them the Book and
the Balance, that the people might dispense justice; and We sent down
Iron, in which there is violent force and also uses for the People, and
(We did so also) in order that Allah might know who would help Him
and His messengers in the unseen; verily Allah is strong, sublime"
(57:25). For Shaltut, the mention of iron is crucial and encourages the
development of industry, especially for the sake of defense.[45]

Finally, the Qur'an deals with certain aspects of the practice of
warfare. Most of these deal with exemptions from military service,
the necessity of declarations of war, army discipline, and the like.
Only one heading (out of fourteen) deals with the issue of interest to
this essay. Discussing prisoners of war, Shaltut quotes Qur'an 8:67: "It
is not for a prophet to have prisoners so as to cause havoc in the
land," and comments:

When the [leader of the Muslims] has caused havoc in the land
and when the taking of captives has been allowed to him, he may

choose between liberating them out of kindness without any ransom or compensation and taking ransom from them, which may consist of property or men. The choice must be made on the basis of what he sees as the common interest. "So when you meet those who have disbelieved, let there be slaughter until when you have made havoc of them, bind them fast, then liberate them out of kindness or in return for ransom" (Qur'an 47:4).[46]

With respect to the *jus in bello*, Shaltut's treatise is unsatisfying. Yet the preoccupation of the text with the *jus ad bellum* fits with his purpose. It also, I suggest, suits his political standing in the Egyptian state. As the Shaykh al-Azhar, Shaltut was required to play a certain role in Egypt; that role involves setting forth the general rules governing the use of force in Islam. It does not involve a serious engagement with the particulars of military strategy, such as al-Shaybani's treatise exhibits.

My example of a revolutionary treatise is also from Egypt. The tract entitled *Al-Faridah al-Ghai'bah*, advertised as the "Creed of Sadat's Assassins," is a fascinating text in many respects.[47] Its greatest importance lies in its argument for the necessity of fighting in pursuit of an Islamic state and in its refusal to accept any "in between" solutions to the problem of forming an Islamic polity. Those rulers who attempt to implement a "mixed regime" in which laws derived from Islamic and non-Islamic sources form an amalgam of norms are apostates and should be killed. Similarly, those who support these rulers in their apostasy should be killed. The point of fighting is the formation of an Islamic polity, which ought to be universal.

Again, the preoccupation of the text is with the *jus ad bellum*. Two sections (out of one hundred and forty) deal with issues of discrimination in war. In the first, the author cites two versions of the *hadith* in which the Prophet, informed of the deaths of women and children during a night raid, says, "They are from them." The author comments: "This means: when they [Muslim soldiers] do not do it on purpose without need for it (it is allowed to kill these dependents)."[48]

The second section cites two *hadith* reports in which the Prophet forbids the killing of women, children, and old men. The author comments simply: "The previous Tradition ... concerning the permissibility of killing dependents does not contradict this Tradition inasmuch as the situation in each Tradition is different from the other."[49]

We may explain the relative lack of development of this point in one of two ways: either the author is uninterested in the *jus in bello* or is not actively engaged with military affairs in such a way that the kind of cases that would lead to a fuller development of *jus in bello* considerations become the object of reflection. I think we must opt for the latter. It is typical of much twentieth-century Islamic thought that it is not involved with considerations of statecraft. The planning and implementation of military strategy, as other aspects of political life, have by and large not been the province of Islamic thinkers in the last two centuries. Islamic thought has been either in the position of providing legitimacy, and perhaps general guidance, to a leadership that has generally been authoritarian and more concerned with modernization than Islamization; or it has been in the position of opposing such leadership—in one author's terms, it has been a language of resistance.[50]

The War Between Iran and Iraq

It is only very recently that this factor has begun to change. With the formation of the Islamic Republic of Iran, we have a state that is in some sense attempting to implement Islamic norms in all phases of social and political life. Not least important in this is the way Iranian leaders developed policy in the war with Iraq. While we need not repeat the analysis of that conflict offered in chapter 3, the following points are worth making with respect to the *jus in bello* in contemporary Islam.

First, Iran's leaders defined the war in Islamic terms. Khumayni interpreted the war as a defense of Islamic territory against a secular (and therefore corrupt) Iraqi aggressor. Saddam Hussein, in particular, was characterized as an apostate: one who was once a Muslim but has somehow departed from the faith.

Second, Iran's leaders spoke of their policy as "Islamic warfare."[51] In that regard, they thought it important to discriminate between the guilty Iraqi leadership and the innocent (or at least, not so guilty) people of Iraq. The Iranian leadership viewed the Iraqis as oppressed people who would, once they understood the circumstances of war (that is, Iraq had committed aggression against Iran), take the opportunity to rise up against Saddam Hussein and his Baathist collaborators. Eventually, the people of Iraq would follow the Iranian path and establish an Islamic government. Hashemi Rafsanjani, then Speaker of the Majlis (or Parliament), said, "We think that in the future, when an Islamic or people's government is set up in Iraq, . . . that will be more useful for the people of Iraq who remain."[52]

The point was that the war was not equally against all Iraqis. Some attempt to discriminate between targets thus followed. According to Khumayni, the Iranian military was to do "nothing to harm the cities which have no defence."[53] In a 1982 speech honoring Iran's Revolutionary Guards, Khumayni recalled the initial strikes of the

Iranian air force into Iraq. He noted that they destroyed numerous military targets and said they could have done far more damage "were it not for their Islamic commitment and their desire to protect the innocent and their fear of destroying property belonging to the brotherly Iraqi nation—a fact which still inhibits them."[54]

In the same vein, it is interesting to note the conclusions of the U.N. Security Council's report on "Prisoners of War in Iran and Iraq."[55] Both sides had been accused of violating international standards concerning the treatment of prisoners. While the mission dispatched by the Secretary General did not entirely clear Iran of accusations of physical abuse, it held the characteristic Iranian offense to be "ideological abuse." According to the report, prisoners were divided into "loyalists" (those defending the Iraqi regime) and "believers" (who indicated their support for an Islamic polity). The latter were given special favors, which created an atmosphere of tension in the POW camps administered by Iran and eventually led to rioting in some of the camps. Assuming the accuracy of the report, one might say that Iranian treatment of POWs reflected the sense that the Iraqi people would be open to "liberation" from the oppressive regime of Saddam Hussein, as well as the notion that Iran should encourage this openness.

Eventually, Iran seems to have dropped its positive view of the Iraqi people, who did not rush to overthrow Saddam Hussein or the Baathist regime. Chubin and Tripp think that the realization that there would be no quick uprising by the Iraqis contributed to Iran's decision to shell Basra in February 1984. In this interpretation, the shelling would symbolize a growing conviction that the Iraqi people must be held responsible for their continued support of Saddam Hussein. However, the same authors note that Iran's attacks on Iraqi cities may be understood as a policy based on perceptions of military needs: in particular, the need to deter Iraq's own, more comprehensive policy of bombing the civilian population in Iran.

In any case, Iran's acts appear to follow rather closely certain patterns characteristic of classical Islamic thought. The attempt to distinguish degrees of guilt among the enemy population; the notion that those most responsible deserve greater punishment; even the notion that military realities can excuse or justify less discriminate uses of force—all are a part of the classical Islamic *jus in bello*. While much more work needs to be done to fill out the picture presented, it seems clear that, given the proper context, contemporary Muslims, like their classical forebears, understand the Islamic mission to involve the crafting of a politico-military consensus on the conduct of war that respects the moral impulse to distinguish the innocent from the guilty.

Conclusion

One might go on to discuss other examples. But my point, I think, is established. If one wants to understand the Islamic tradition on limiting war, one has to recall that cultural traditions on war, peace, and statecraft are not purely "moral" or even "theological" traditions. The Islamic approach to the conduct of war reflects the moral concern that the just and the unjust, the innocent and the guilty, not be equally subject to the damage of war. In that respect, its concerns are analogous to those of the just war tradition. But the content of justice and injustice, of guilt and innocence, is specified by the interaction of this moral concern with religious, political, and military factors. While just war tradition is similarly formed, the interaction of these factors in the two cultures leads to important differences in the development of the *jus in bello*.

In particular, the recent history of Islamic thought on war indicates that students of ethics ought never to underestimate the importance of a real engagement with statecraft, including military strategy, for the formulation of a developed teaching on the conduct of war. Classical Islamic theorists were in rather a different position from most of their modern counterparts in this regard. No doubt, we shall know more about the meaning of "Islamic warfare" as we learn more about Iranian discussions of the war with Iraq. In the meantime, I think we shall have to recognize that a specifically Islamic contribution to the rules governing the conduct of modern war is still very much in process.

CHAPTER FIVE

Soldiers Without Portfolio: Irregular War in the Tradition of Islam

Consideration of the just war and jihad traditions yields a sense that war is, or ought to be, an activity governed by rules. We have seen, for example, that Islamic thinkers consider the stipulation that wars be fought only for religiously approved purposes to be a way of limiting the occasion and damage of war. Similarly, we have seen that rules governing the conduct of war involve (among other things) an attempt to discriminate between the innocent and the guilty among the enemy.

The notion that war is governed by rules can be challenged in a number of ways. In this chapter, the concern is with the challenge presented by *irregular war*—a phrase used by numerous writers to describe a set of conflicts that, in their very origins and motivation, appear to deny important aspects of the just war and jihad traditions. Rebellions, revolutions, "people's war," are all held to be irregular, primarily because they challenge the traditions' stipulation that the right to wage war belongs to publicly constituted, recognized political authorities. Waged at least in part by forces that fight against rather than for such authorities, the wars of "soldiers without portfolio" present an important challenge for traditions that try to integrate moral concern with the use of lethal force. The desire to limit the occasion and the damage of war, it seems, is best served by restricting the right of war to established authorities. But the desire for justice may not be.

As in other chapters, I begin with an illustration from just war thought. In this case, a little-known yet undeniably important example from the U.S. Civil War will serve to clarify the possibilities and problems for just war tradition in dealing with the phenomenon of wars fought by soldiers without portfolio. Following that discussion, I turn to examples from classical and contemporary Islam.

On the Idea of Irregular War

It requires the power of the Almighty and a whole century to grow an oak tree; but only a pair of arms, an ax, and an hour or two to cut it down.[1]

Many memorable lines have been written about the American Civil War. From the standpoint of the study of ethics, however, no statement is more suggestive than the one quoted above, which was composed by a German immigrant named Francis Lieber. Legal adviser to the Union General Henry Wager Halleck, Lieber was the primary author of *General Orders No. 100*—a document that, in its applications of international law to the War Between the States, constitutes a landmark attempt to relate the just war tradition to modern conflict. Lieber had a strong sense of that tradition and thought it an essential aspect of Western civilization. It is not surprising, then, that he saw aspects of the fighting between Union and Confederate armies as problematic.

As Lieber put it, just war thinking attempts to apply a noble sentiment: "Men who take up arms against one another in public war do not cease on that account to be moral beings, responsible to one another and to God."[2] The War Between the States presented a threat to that precept, however. As both Lieber and General Halleck saw it, some of those fighting were arrogating to themselves the right to transgress the rules of war. Halleck put it this way:

The rebel authorities claim the right to send men, in the garb of peaceful citizens, to waylay and attack our troops, to burn bridges and houses and to destroy property and persons within our lines. They demand that such persons be treated as ordinary belligerents, and that when captured they have extended to them the same rights as other prisoners of war; they also threaten that if such persons be punished as marauders and spies they will retaliate by executing our prisoners of war in their possession.[3]

For Lieber, "public war" involved the engagement of armed men, authorized to carry and use their weapons by a recognized political authority, identified as combatants by a public sign (uniforms, e.g.), who distinguished the enemy's fighting forces from its civilians, and (ideally) followed notions of justice in dealing with enemy captives, property, and the like. The armies of the "rebel forces" challenged all of these notions. They thus, by their "irregular" status and behavior, challenged the traditions of justice in war and prompted Lieber's comment.

What is the status of soldiers who fight an irregular war? According to Lieber, such soldiers are a threat to the tradition of just and limited warfare built up through the history of Western civilization. First, they lack "right authority" to make war, in the sense that they do not represent a sovereign political community—in modern terms, a nation-state. Second, they engage in such nonconventional tactics as deception (e.g., wearing civilian clothing), attacks upon civilian targets, assassination and hostage taking. Such "fighting men" are not soldiers in any traditional sense. As Lieber put it, they "unite the four-fold character of the spy, the brigand, the assassin, and the rebel."[4] Such characterizations lend themselves to the judgment that irregular soldiers are criminals and the wars they fight are actually large-scale examples of murder or theft.

At this point, Lieber's arguments were reminiscent of a long-standing assumption in Western discussions of justice and war. Historically speaking, as James Turner Johnson puts it, "just war limits do not apply in war against rebels."[5] Throughout the history of Western reflection on war, rebels or "soldiers without portfolio" have been regarded as a threat to the foundations of established political order and the stability it represents. To cite a particularly famous example, Martin Luther saw the Peasants' Rebellion of 1524–1525 as a battle between the forces of anarchy (the peasants) and of order (the German nobility). He thus argued that allowing peasant armies to dictate terms of justice to the nobles would undermine an established set of institutions, without presenting any real replacement for them. No matter how just their complaints, a peasants' victory would mean lawlessness, disorder, bloodshed, and suffering. Thus the rebels should be treated not as soldiers but as criminals, and Luther urged the nobility to employ their armies to "stab, kill, and strangle" the peasants as though they were rabid beasts.[6]

Lieber understood the logic of this position. Indeed, at certain points he and his colleagues characterized the threat posed by southern rebels to established conventions of war in terms almost as bleak as Luther's. Not only do Confederate irregulars unite in themselves "the fourfold character of the spy, the brigand, the assassin, and the rebel," as we have seen. According to Lieber, their pernicious behavior can be characterized even more concretely: "That to-day passes you in the garb and mien of a peaceful citizen, may to-morrow, as a guerrillaman, fire your house or murder you from behind the hedge."[7] To treat such fighters as soldiers is difficult. It weighs against the interests of real soldiers at every point. Those in the field worry that the practice of dis-

criminating between military and civilian targets will cost them their
lives. Those making strategy fear that the morale of their troops will
suffer and popular support for their efforts will wane. Finally, those
who care about the tradition of just and limited war worry that the
gradual erosion of its standards will result in wars fought only by General Sherman's dictum: War is hell. In hell, there can be no limit to suffering. In war, there can be; but that is only true insofar as fighting
forces are willing to adhere to the fragile network of restraints worked
out by previous generations.

In the end, however, Lieber's concern for justice in war led him to
an important innovation in the tradition that he valued so much—an
innovation that is now part of the formal tradition of international law.
Considering that any realistic assessment of human affairs must deal
with the fact that there are times when people feel constrained to use
force *against* an established government, as well as for it, Lieber concluded that "just rebellion" cannot be an oxymoron. Luther and others
might be right in expressing a presumption against rebellion. A just
war thinker should worry about such questions as "Who will govern
once an established regime is overthrown?" or, "What will rebels do
the day *after* the revolution has come?" Yet the presumption against irregulars cannot be absolute. Even Luther recognized that, in cases of
extreme and long-standing deprivation or oppression, there must be
room for an uprising. And in the particular case confronted by Lieber—
the War Between the States—the issue of political sovereignty was un-
certain enough to inspire doubt in his lawyer's mind. After all, many
argued, prior to the war, that the various states did have a right to se-
cede from the Union. One *might* consider, then, that the Confederacy,
with its institutions of government, economy, and law *did* constitute a
sovereign political authority. And, if that were so, those fighting on the
southern side could reasonably consider themselves "regular soldiers,"
authorized to fight by their government.

For these reasons, Lieber argued that one could not always follow
the tradition in equating rebels and criminals. Citizens have a right to
protect themselves and their property, even when their enemy is an established government. Lieber thus suggested that the line dividing irregulars from criminality should be drawn less in terms of "right
authority" than of *jus in bello* standards like proportionality and discrimination. The "guerrillamen" of the Confederacy would be treated
as soldiers, unless they engaged in murder or the killing of prisoners—
behaviors for which even uniformed officers of the Union army might
suffer punishment.

Lieber's innovation is now a part of the modern law of war.
"Guerrillas," "freedom fighters," and "armies of liberation" are treated

like regular soldiers. Changes in the law do not, however, do away with the moral and political difficulties attached to the phenomenon of "irregular war." Whom do irregulars represent? By what authority do they fight? How should existing governments respond? And what about Lieber's continuing concern for *jus in bello* restraints? As irregulars see it, the success or failure of their cause often depends on engaging in tactics that are beyond the bounds of the laws of war. They justify such nonconventional tactics as assassination, terrorism, and hostage taking as a way of dealing with the numerical and technological superiority enjoyed by the regular forces. Yet, if the "regular" forces feel their lives endangered or their cause threatened by the irregulars' tactics, will they not respond in kind? In this way, irregulars may yet prove blameworthy, in that they introduce "a system of barbarity which becomes intenser in its demoralization as it spreads and is prolonged."[8] One might say that Lieber extended the rights of war to irregular fighters. But how does one extend to them a sense of the duties imposed on soldiers by the tradition of just and limited war? Despite Lieber's legal innovation, the moral presumption against irregulars seems to remain, largely for the reasons indicated in his dictum: In their tendency to justify violations of the rules of war, irregulars threaten to lay the ax to the fragile, yet beautiful traditions by which Western civilization attempts to limit the brutality of war.

Irregular War and Islamic Thought

Throughout its long history, Islam too has dealt with the problem of irregular war. Yet discussions of irregular war in Islam are unique. In the classical period, one finds a heavy presumption against rebellion, revolution, and the like, based partly on deep worries about disruption of an established political order. At the same time, one finds no materials that suggest an attitude like that of Luther or that "just war [in this case, jihad] limits do not apply to rebels."[9] Indeed, "regular Muslim forces" are to be more limited in their response to rebels than to the "people of war" in the conduct of the "normal" jihad. This feature of Islamic reflection is quite striking and, as I shall indicate, rests on a combination of particular instances of irregular war and religious reasoning.

Even more striking, however, are the reflections presented by certain modern Muslims. Indeed, it is these reflections that give, or ought to give, a thoughtful Westerner the most pause in thinking about Islam and irregular war. There is no shortage of Muslim groups currently fighting without official authorization and willing to use nonconventional tactics; that much is hardly news. Yet a close examination of the rationale of these groups raises a question not unlike that posed by Lieber's Confederate "guerrillamen." As Lieber put it, international law considers "that the rising of the people to repel invasion entitles them to the full benefits of the laws of war."[10] In the case of modern Islam, some of the most notorious examples of irregular war may not be such, according to this criterion. From a certain perspective, they are better characterized as a "peoples' struggle" to regain rights of territory and property that have been wrongly taken by invaders. To put it another way: If territory historically identified as "Islamic" (the *dar al-islam*) comes to be dominated by non-Islamic regimes, are Muslims who resist "rebels" and "irregulars"—or are they fighters whose authorization rests in a divine imperative: to command good and forbid evil; to establish a balance between peace, order, and justice in the earth?

Classical Perspectives

Systematic reflection on irregular war in Islam developed, as much of the rest of Islamic political thought, in conjunction with the interests and policies of the Abbasid caliphate. In this regard, al-Shaybani's discussion of questions related to rebels (*ahkam al-bughat*, the "judgments related to rebels," as the jurists called it) is as important a source on irregular war as on the "normal" jihad—that is, the struggle to extend the territory of Islam. We have already seen that one of the primary sources for al-Shaybani's reflections on rebellion were reports concerning the actions of Ali, son-in-law of the Prophet and leader of the Muslims from 656 C.E. until his death by an assassin's knife in 661. For al-Shaybani (and indeed for most Muslim opinion of his time), Ali's rule marked a crucial point in the history of Islam. It was, they said, the time of the first *fitna*, or "testing," of the Muslims, when the community divided into factions over the question of leadership. The precise causes and order of events in the *fitna* were matters of considerable dispute among the Muslims of al-Shaybani's time. Small wonder, since depending on the facts of the case, entire regimes could be declared illegitimate, various groups classified as heretics, and larger than life historical figures consigned to paradise or hell. Nevertheless a brief account is in order and could be constructed as follows.

In the year 656 C.E., the caliph Uthman was killed. Third leader of the Muslims after the Prophet's death, Uthman came to power in 644 following the death of Umar, the great organizer of the early Islamic conquests. Uthman thus assumed the mantle of ruler of an empire, with the attendant powers and problems.

Uthman proceeded to lead the Muslims in the manner of a man who prefers to delegate responsibility rather than to take it upon himself. In some ways, this was unavoidable. The conquests of the Muslims in the first generation after Muhammad were striking, by any measure: first Syria and Palestine, then Egypt, then most of Iraq fell before the armies of the Muslims. It would have been impossible to administer such an empire without the assignment of responsibilities to territorial governors. Indeed, one must assume that a number of the difficulties that led to the *fitna* resulted from the pressure for change exerted by imperial responsibilities upon the thinking and behavior of the Arabs, a people traditionally organized in terms of the more "local" associations of family and clan. Uthman's pattern in delegating responsibility followed the traditional models. He assigned power to members of his clan, the Marwanids, and trusted them to administer their realms according to the practices of Arab tribal chieftains.

Such governance did not fully accord with the new realities imposed by the empire, however. Even more, the assignment of responsibilities on the basis of family and clan did not recognize the new realities imposed on Arab practice by the turn to Islam. Muhammad respected the virtues of traditional Arab life. Indeed, he is supposed to have said, "The best among you [Arabs] in the times before Islam will also be the best among you [Muslims]."[11] The force of such a saying is to play down the difference between Arab traditions and Muslim piety. Uthman's pattern of administration assumed this point of view.

At the same time, the Qur'an clearly declared: "The foremost among you will be the foremost in piety [*taqwa*]" (49:13). The overall thrust of the Qur'an, as of Muhammad's leadership, implied that distinctions in status could not be tied to family and clan relationships or considerations of wealth. The Islamic community was a new type of social organization, in which "the best" from Arab tradition should be preserved, but only insofar as it accorded with considerations of piety. For a man like Ali, who remembered that some of the most severe resistance to Muhammad's preaching had come from the great Arab families, this was a critical point, as it was for many others whose status was founded less on Arab tradition, more on commitment to the new community founded by the Prophet.

With such tensions, conflict was perhaps inevitable. A group of Muslims living on the Egyptian "frontier" of the empire made their way to Medina to complain to Uthman of unjust acts by his appointed governor. At this point, the story becomes extremely murky—Uthman evidently assured the group of his sympathy for them and sent them off with promises to do justice. On their return, however, the group intercepted a messenger, ostensibly sent by the caliph to warn his relatives concerning the danger posed by the malefactors. Their worst fears confirmed, the group now felt that the corruption extended beyond the administration on the frontier and into the heart of Medina itself. Returning to the city, they killed the caliph and made their escape.

This incident set off a series of conflicts in which Ali was at the center. How would the new caliph deal with the murderers of Uthman? The old Arab families, particularly Uthman's clan, waited for justice. So did those who, sympathetic with the complaint of the "frontiersmen," hoped for a regime based more on the Qurʾan than on Arab tradition. Ali moved slowly, biding his time between the two groups. His hope seems to have been to find a way to preserve the unity of the Muslims without resort to arms. Eventually time ran out: Muʿawiya, governor of Syria and a clansman of Uthman, declared Ali unfit to rule and positioned himself to lead the empire. Forced to a military response, Ali led his army to the brink of battle with Muʿawiya's forces. Suddenly the latter proposed a way of mediating the conflict. In a dramatic moment, Muslim historians tell of Muʿawiya's soldiers advancing to the field with copies of the Qurʾan impaled on their lances. Shouting "Let the Qurʾan decide!" they appealed to Ali's piety, and he took the opportunity for peaceful resolution. Unfortunately negotiations ended in a stalemate. Both sides withdrew, and certain of Ali's followers, dissatisfied with this state of affairs, went so far as to declare themselves no longer interested in either leader's claims. "We have no leader but God," they said, and established themselves as a third party, known to history as Kharijites (technically, al-khawarij, from the Arabic word "to exit"). All the factions for the fitna were now present; Ali's position had gone from bad to worse, as he dealt with not one but two groups of rebels—Muʿawiya, representing Arab traditions with all the power of the governor of Syria, and the Kharijites, representing the interests of those desiring full implementation of the new order envisioned by the Qurʾan.

In this situation, Ali acted in ways that established precedents for al-Shaybani and scholars like him. What does one do, faced with rebels on all sides? As noted, the traditional response of Western thought advised: Suppress the rebellion. Restore order first; ask questions after. Ali's approach, reflected in the following reports, was rather different.

> [A contemporary of Ali said:] I entered the Mosque of Kufa through the Kinda gates where I met five men cursing [the caliph] Ali [b. Abi Talib]. One of them, covered with a burnus, said: "I have made a covenant with God that I shall kill him." Whereupon, I kept close [to this man] while his companions dispersed, and I took him to Ali and said: "I heard this man saying that he has made a covenant with God that he will kill you." "Bring him nearer [to me]," said [Ali] and added: "woe to you, who are you?"

"I am Sawwar al-Manquri," replied the man. "Let him go," said
Ali. Thereupon, I said: "Shall I let him go, though [he said that] he
made a covenant with God to kill you?" "Shall I kill him even
though he has not [yet] killed me?" replied Ali. "He has cursed
you," [said I]. "You should then curse him or leave him," said Ali.

It has been related . . . that while [the caliph] Ali b. Abi Talib was
once making a sermon on Friday, [some] Kharijis, from one side of
the Mosque, pronounced the formula: "Judgment belongs to none
save God." "A word of Truth to which is given a false meaning,"
said Ali [and he added]: "we shall not prohibit you from entering
our mosques to mention His [God's] name; we shall not deny you
[your share of] the fayʾ, so long as you join hands with us; nor
shall we fight you until you attack us.". . .

It has also been related . . . that [the caliph] Ali b. Abi Talib said in
the Battle of the Camel: "Whoever flees [from us] shall not be
chased, no [Muslim] prisoner of war shall be killed, no wounded
in battle shall be dispatched, no enslavement [of women and chil-
dren] shall be allowed, and no property [of a Muslim] shall be
confiscated."[12]

Such reports bear close examination. They indicate, first and
foremost, that whatever else a rebel may be, he (or she) remains a
Muslim and must be treated as such. The last of the reports is particularly instructive here. Recalling our earlier discussion of the ways
Muslim thinkers worked out the meaning of discrimination in war,
one is reminded that considerations of one's acceptance or rejection of
the basic tenets of Islam are crucial in determining one's rights. The
treatment prescribed for non-Muslim combatants is rather different
from that set forth by Ali; in particular, Muslim rebels taken as prisoners of war must not be killed, and no rebel is to lose his or her property
as a result of war.

Further, the resort to violence against rebels is more tightly governed than in the case of jihad to expand the territory of Islam. As Ali
says to the Kharijites in the mosque: "nor shall we fight you until you
attack us." Response to rebels, it seems, must be commensurate to their
action in a way not characteristic of other conflicts. According to al-
Shaybani, for example, a just cause for war exists whenever the people
of the territory of war refuse the summons to submit to Islamic rule.
Resort to war against rebels, on the other hand, requires that the rebels
themselves initiate hostilities. It is not even sufficient to know that
rebels intend to attack, if and when they think themselves able to over-
come the established regime. Unless the rebel party actually resorts to

violence, the caliph must measure his response: "Shall I kill him even though he has not [yet] killed me?" replied Ali. . . ."You should then curse him or leave him."

Finally, Ali's comments—and even more, his practice—suggest that the goal of action against rebels is different from that of the war to extend the frontiers of Islam. According to one author, "the primary purpose [of a war against Muslim rebels] is the reconciliation of the contending parties and not the punishment or elimination of the dissenters. . . . Vengeance or oppression should play no role in suppressing the rebellion of" Muslim dissenters.[13] In this sense, Ali's practice—and indeed the entire approach of classical jurists to the problem of rebellion—might be seen as a response to Qur'an 49:9–10:

> If two parties of believers fall to fighting, then make peace between them. And if one party of them does wrong to the other, fight the one that does wrong until it returns to the way of Allah; then, if it returns, make peace between them with justice, and act equitably. Lo! Allah loves those who act equitably. The believers are brothers: so make peace between your brothers and observe your duty to Allah, that you may receive mercy.

Of course, such an injunction "cuts both ways." If, as Ali saw, the duty to "make peace" required the caliph to make resort to war truly the last of his options, it must also be true that dissenters should try to resolve their grievances against established authority by means short of violence. Any act of rebellion risks the peace of the Muslim community; there must then be a way of distinguishing "just rebellion" from other, less legitimate acts of violence against the established government.

It is here that al-Shaybani and other classical theorists join the discussion. Reflecting on Ali's example, they understood what a Muslim ruler, motivated by piety and responsibility for the welfare of the Muslim community, should do when faced with challenges to his authority. He should, above all, respect the fact that his opponents are Muslims. Paraphrasing Lieber's summary of the just war tradition, we might say that the ruler of the Muslims should follow the maxim that "Muslims who take up arms against one another in public war do not cease on that account to be members of a community, responsible to God and the example of the Prophet."

At the same time, a caliph who waits too long, or is too measured in his response, risks the welfare of the entire community. Again reflecting on the example of Ali, classical jurists knew that his noble and pious policy had failed to forestall civil war—that the son-in-law of the Prophet met his death on the blade of a dissident assassin's knife, giving rise to twenty years of civil strife that resulted in the establishment of a dynasty founded by Mu'awiya and his sons. Classical jurists by and large viewed this consequence, and indeed the entire *fitna*, as a tragic development and drew the following lesson: It may be that there is such thing as a "just rebellion." It is certainly true that Muslims can have legitimate reasons to complain about the injustice of particular regimes or rulers. But it is also true that revolutionaries rarely achieve the goals they seek. In particular, the Kharijites, withdrawing from both Ali and Mu'awiya, came to be seen as a paradigm for the type of rebels who care more for ideals than for the common good. Like Ali, classical theorists saw in the Kharijites' insistence "We have no king but God" a "word of Truth to which is given a false meaning." They thus applauded Ali's example, yet insisted there must be a heavy burden of proof upon those who would make a just revolution. To that end, they developed a set of criteria to distinguish several types of uprisings: rebellions, for which Ali's example held good; "spreading corruption," in which the (so-called) rebels are really "highwaymen," that is, brigands; and apostasy, in which persons or groups act in ways characteristic of treason.

The spirit of the classical jurists' approach to irregular war can be illustrated by the following *hadith*.

> Auf b. Malik al-Ashja'i reported God's messenger as saying, "Your best [leaders] are those whom you like and who like you, on whom you invoke blessings and who invoke blessings on you; and your worst [leaders] are those whom you hate and who hate you, whom you curse and who curse you." They asked God's messenger whether in that event they should not depose them, but he replied, "No, as long as they observe the prayer among you; no, as long as they observe the prayer among you. If anyone has a governor whom he sees doing anything which is an act of disobedience to God, he must disapprove of the disobedience to God which he commits, but must never withdraw from obedience."

> Ibn Umar reported God's messenger as saying, "Hearing and obeying are the duty of a Muslim man both regarding what he likes and what he dislikes, as long as he is not commanded to perform an act of disobedience to God, in which case he must neither hear nor obey."

> Abu Huraira reported the Prophet as saying, "The B. Israil [i.e., the Jews] were governed by the prophets, as often as one died another taking his place. There will be no prophet after me, but there will be numerous caliphs." He was asked what command he had

to give and replied, "Fulfil the oath of allegiance to each and give them their due, for God will question them about what He asked them to guard."[14]

When is rebellion justified? The answer is, almost never. No doubt, there are some rulers that a Muslim will "like," that is, will consider pious and just, and others that a Muslim will consider less so. Nevertheless there is no justification for deposing the latter, so long as they fulfill the basic obligations of a member of the Muslim community—for example, "they observe the prayer among you." Any member of the Muslim community can and should criticize an unjust ruler. But he "must never withdraw from obedience"—that is, engage in active insurrection.

Again, one must obey the commands of the person in authority, even if one does not like them. "Hearing and obeying are the duty of a Muslim man." The sole exception comes in the case of a command that involves disobedience to God. It is important, however, that the reports cited do not go on to say, "When this exception occurs, the ruler should be overthrown." As the Islamic theorists had it, Muslims faced with an illegal or immoral command must "omit to obey." The injustice of the command does not, in itself, justify revolutionary activity.

Finally, the problem of unjust rulers is dealt with by referring judgment to God. God established those in authority, and it is the part of others to obey. If rulers are unjust, then they, like other sinners, will ultimately find punishment with God: "God will question them about what He asked them to guard." To depose rulers, to engage in active insurrection, is to arrogate to oneself the role of God. There is, in short, a heavy burden of proof upon Muslims who would engage in "just rebellion."

How, then, does it become possible to fight against an unjust caliph? According to the jurists, those who would be considered rebels rather than criminals or traitors must meet three conditions.[15]

First, there must be an act of resistance to the ruler or his designated representatives. This act, called al-khuruj, may be of several types. One might, for example, refuse to pay taxes. One might also kill the tax collector. At one level, this is an obvious condition—without such behavior, who would even speak of active rebellion or insurrection? The theorists' point may be seen, however, when one considers their insistence that al-khuruj does not include public criticism of established authority. For a rebellion to exist, resistance must go beyond speech or "merely" expressive activity (e.g., a peaceful demonstration). A rebel is one who expressly violates laws or policies of an established regime—this is the meaning of al-khuruj.

Second, the rebel cause must be based on *al-ta'wil*. In its ordinary sense, this term refers to the interpretation of Islamic sources (the Qur'an or the reports of Prophetic words and deeds). The point thus seems to be that the rebels have a just (i.e., Islamically legitimate) cause for their action. Alternatively, one could say their citation of Islamic sources in support of insurrection indicates a right (again, Islamically legitimate) intention on the rebels' part.

For classical thinkers, the Kharijites provided an important example for this requirement. To say "We have no king but God" or "Judgment belongs to none save God" is to make the case for rebellion in *Islamic* terms. To appreciate the point, one must remember that rebellion was by definition a war between Muslims. One might imagine cases of insurrection in which a group resisting the caliph cited as justification that it did not wish to live under an Islamic government. Such insurrections would not meet the technical requirements for a rebellion. The caliph could then respond to such a group in very different—usually less measured—ways. For many jurists, the primary examples of non-Islamic insurrections were cases of apostasy. To cite the most famous of these: Following the death of Muhammad in 632 C.E. Abu Bakr became the leader of the Muslims. Certain groups in the Arabian peninsula then refused to pay *zakat*, a type of "charity tax" established by the Qur'an as an obligation for Muslims, to the agents of the new caliph. These groups did not, according to our sources, renounce the faith taught by Muhammad—they remained believers in one God. They did, however, refuse to remit the "charity tax" to Muhammad's successor. Abu Bakr, we are told, interpreted this as a claim that the payment of *zakat* was not incumbent upon Muslims—in effect, a public denial of one of the basic tenets of Islam. He therefore made war upon the tribes in question, forcing them to pay the obligatory tax.

For classical thinkers, the usefulness of this example was as follows. *Al-ta'wil*, or the interpretation cited by rebels, cannot include a renunciation or rejection of basic Islamic duties. A rebel cannot refuse to pay *zakat*, then cite as a reason that the charity tax is not a duty for Muslims. Similarly, he cannot refuse to pay, then cite as a reason that the Qur'an is not the Word of God. Such a person is an apostate, not a rebel. According to Islamic law, he is to be jailed and, if he does not repent, must be executed.

Apostasy aside, the requirement of *al-ta'wil* raises other problems. Recall again the Kharijites and their confrontation with Ali: "Judgment belongs to none save God. . . . A word of Truth to which is given a false meaning." Suppose a group, engaged in insurrection, cites an Islamic text as justification, but its interpretation of the text is wrong. Must rebels be correct in their interpretation of Islamic sources? The problem is significant, given that there is a presumption against rebellion, and given that many rebel groups (e.g., the Kharijites) represented a minority point of view among the Muslims. With this in mind, it is interesting that most Islamic thinkers argued that, ultimately, the rightness or wrongness of the rebels' *taʾwil* is not significant. What is significant is that their interpretation not be "frivolous"; a student of Western ethics or law would probably say that the rebels' rationale must be conscientious, or that the rebels' reasoning shows signs of a serious attempt to understand the sources they appeal to.

The third requirement for rebels is that they demonstrate a sizable and organized membership. Termed *al-shauka* by the jurists, this requirement relates primarily to the concern that the notion of just rebellion not become license for anarchic behavior. In effect, one might see it as an attempt to deal with the problem of authorization. No one person constitutes a rebel force—in fact, most jurists go on to say that a group of ten cannot constitute such a force. It is important to note that the jurists are not making a pragmatic point here. Their concern is not that a single person or a group of ten cannot be effective against the forces of the government. The jurists' worry is that, since the rebels constitute, by definition, a fighting force that does not have authorization by the existing regime, they must indicate a significant level of support within the Muslim community. One thinks again of Francis Lieber and the problem of irregular war: Since the just war tradition presupposes that armies fight in the service of (or by the authorization of) publicly recognized governments, a rebel force seems to be unjust, by definition. Yet international law recognizes the right of a people to rise "en masse" to defend their interests. It is possible then for irregular forces to find their authorization in terms of a claim to defend the interests of "the people."

In the Muslim case, the requirement of *al-shauka* seems to be a way to say that a group of Muslim rebels may have legitimacy, provided their size and strength indicate significant support from the Muslim community. In addition, *al-shauka* requires that the rebels demonstrate that they are organized and have identifiable leadership. The point seems clear enough: Rebels are not a "ragtag" group; they are not engaged in a temporary or largely spontaneous activity like rioting. They are organized "for the long haul"; they have considerable support within the Muslim community; they have, as has already been said, engaged in active resistance to the established authorities and are able to cite an Islamic rationale in support of their activities.

Those groups, and only those groups, who satisfy these three criteria are to be classified and treated as rebels, according to the jurists. Others may meet one or more of the criteria. Apostates, for example,

may engage in active resistance and even have an organized following. Without an Islamic rationale, however, they are not "rebels," and
the caliph is not obliged to respond in the measured way exemplified
by Ali in his dealings with the Kharijites. Similarly, a small group with
its base in a mountain region might kidnap or kill agents of the government. Such a group might even provide an Islamic rationale in support of its activities. If it cannot demonstrate a certain breadth of
support among the Muslims, however, its members are not rebels.
They are "highwaymen" who "spread corruption in the earth" and are
subject to criminal prosecution and punishment.

Following these examples, one can understand the reasoning of
the jurists in terms of the problem of authorization. "Rebels," one
might say, functions as a technical term that, when applied, confers a
certain legitimacy of status on a group actively engaged in opposition
to an established government. More precisely, one might say that the
term protects the members of the group by suggesting that they remain Muslims, thus imposing certain obligations on the caliph and
his armed forces.

What one misses in the discussion, however, is a notion of limits
on the means employed by rebels. Recall that Lieber's concern with
the Confederate rebels dealt not only with questions of authorization
but with guerrilla tactics: deception, failure to distinguish combatants
and noncombatants, assassination, and hostage taking all had a place
in the Confederate strategy of irregular war. Those who used such tactics violated the standards of just and limited war, even if one could
make a case for the rebels' legitimacy as part of a popular uprising.

Classical jurists are surprisingly silent on this issue. In his seminal discussion of the topic, Khaled Abou El Fadl flatly states: "The
bughat [rebels] are not responsible for any destruction of property or
life if such destruction occurs in the course of the rebellion."[16] There is
no formal criterion equivalent to *al-khuruj*, *al-taʾwil*, or *al-shauka* that indicates any special concern with the rebels' attempt to discriminate between innocent and guilty, or with their observance of rules governing
the treatment of prisoners of war. One can only speculate on the reasons for this omission. Does it, for example, result from the realistic
perception that rebel forces, which will almost always be at a disad-
vantage in a battlefield situation, will often feel justified or excused in
violating the customary rules of engagement? Whatever the case, jurists who place special restrictions on the behavior of the caliph, while
placing none on the conduct of the rebel forces, appear to be giving the
advantage to the latter.

As Abou El Fadl notes, however, the basic criteria for determining whether a group has the status of "rebels" do seem to impose a

few limits on the group's behavior.[17] While these are not the object of discussion apart from the criteria already discussed, they are neverthe-less important in the general discussion of classical Islamic approaches to irregular war.

First, in conjunction with the notion of *al-shauka* (i.e., that a rebel group must demonstrate a following and some semblance of organiza-tion), classical writers were able to say that members of the group who act independently did not do so as rebels (i.e., did not sustain their pro-tected status, and could be tried as apostates or criminals). The point re-lates to Abou El Fadl's stipulation that the rebels are not responsible for their destructive acts "if such destruction occurs in the course of the re-bellion." The most-discussed case seems to have been the assassination of Ali: since the act was performed by a single member of the Kharijite group, it was not a part of the general rebellion and was therefore not a protected act. Indeed, since most acts of assassination by rebels are per-formed by solitary individuals or small groups of fighters, one might imagine this as a way of saying that assassination is almost always wrong. In a slightly later period than we are discussing (eleventh cen-tury), when the rebels known to history as the Order of Assassins gained a widespread reputation for terrorizing their enemies through assassinating leading political figures from their bases in Iran and Syria, the judgment that rebels acting individually, "under cloak of darkness" as it were, are acting illegitimately, seems to have played a part in the almost universal rejection of the Assassins' cause.[18]

A second limitation on the tactics of rebels appears in the discus-sion of *al-ta'wil* (the rationale or interpretation on which the rebels' ac-tion is based). According to Abou El Fadl, a "few jurists" questioned the majority judgment concerning the status of the Kharijites. For most, the fact that the Kharijites' slogans were clearly Islamic made them rebels rather than apostates, even though their understanding of Islamic precepts was imperfect. For the few, however, this was not the case. As Abou El Fadl has it, these "argued that since the Khawarij [Kharijites] advocated the indiscriminate slaughter of Muslims they were apostates rather than *bughat* [rebels]."[19] The most interesting fea-ture of this argument, in the light of a concern for limits on rebel tac-tics, lies in the suggestion that the Kharijites' violation of one Islamic precept (that the life and property of Muslims is inviolable) invalidates their claim to be acting as members of the Muslim community. Those who argued this way had in mind historical traditions characterizing the Kharijites as a group of zealots, who felt themselves justified in making judgments on the validity of other persons' professions of faith—the result being that the Kharijites could then execute those held to be insincere, whether or not they posed a military threat. At least for the few, failure to discriminate between the innocent and the guilty seems therefore to have been grounds to dismiss offending groups from the category of rebels.

Such limits, while loosely formulated, indicate something of a concern for appropriate conduct on the part of rebel groups. The remarkable fact of classical Islamic thought on this topic, however, remains its struggle to recognize and regulate the right of rebellion against established authority. Like Francis Lieber (and indeed, most of Western, just war thought), the great Muslim theorists were concerned about the threat to established institutions and traditions (and thus, to human welfare) posed by the actions of irregular fighting forces. Recognizing the fact of injustice in government, however, such theorists could not avoid the conclusion that the antigovernment actions of certain groups had at least *some* legitimacy. More precisely, they could not argue that such groups forfeited their standing as Muslims, with rights that the caliph was duty-bound to protect. They thus struggled to find ways to distinguish "rebellion," with its attendant (although admittedly weak) aura of legitimacy from treason and criminal activity. In so doing, Islamic thinkers prefigured (by nearly a thousand years) Lieber's conclusion that participation in a rebellion does not, in and of itself, make one a criminal. Muslims who take up arms against one another in armed conflict do not cease on that account to be members of a community, responsible to God and the example of the Prophet.

Modern Islam

When one turns to more contemporary conflicts, one is first struck by the relevance of classical reasoning to the 1980s war between Iran and Iraq. When the Ayatullah Khumayni declared that Iranian soldiers were "fighting to protect Islam," and that the Baathist regime in Iraq had, in violating Iran's borders, committed "rebellion by blasphemy against Islam," his terminology suggested the parallel. Iraqi soldiers were, in effect, rebels. Those taken prisoner were not killed— though they were subjected to a form of "ideological pressure" in Iranian POW camps. Similarly, Iraqi noncombatants were seen as dependents of rebels. They were therefore not to be the direct target of aerial bombardment or missile strikes. All of this has been discussed in chapter 4.

With the classical discussion of rebels in mind, however, we can now see more readily the significance of Khumayni's characterization of the Baathist regime as "non-Muslim" and of its policy toward Iran as "rebellion by blasphemy against Islam." One might imagine a debate between Iranian jurists: Are the Iraqi leaders to be classified as

"rebels"? In attacking the Islamic Republic of Iran, they satisfy the criterion of *al-khuruj*—that is, they are engaged in active resistance against
an established, Islamic government. Since there are soldiers fighting in
the name of the Baathist regime, one might imagine it has *al-shauka*,
meaning a sizable and organized following. Yet Iranian leaders were
reluctant to consider the Iraqi soldiers as willing and informed participants in the rebellion. (Hence their policy toward prisoners of war.)
Most important, however, the Baathist regime could not have a *ta'wil*—
a rationale for fighting based on Islamic sources. This was so because of
President Hussein's repeated characterizations of his administration as
"secular"; as based on ethnicity; and his restriction of Islam to the role
of an Arab civil religion. To "rebel by blasphemy" is a euphemism for
apostasy. The suggestion is that Khumayni and others had reached the
conclusion that the planners of the invasion could not be treated as
rebels—they were apostates. In this sense, the resistance to negotiations
with Iraq, the insistence that one result of the war had to be the resigna-
tion of Saddam Hussein, makes sense. For apostates, whose behavior is
equivalent to treason, are the worst of enemies. Thus Khumayni frequently said that his regime would never negotiate with the Iraqis: "To
compromise with oppressors is to oppress. That is contrary to the
views of all the prophets."[20]

Rebels can be wrong, even mistaken in their reasoning. They
nevertheless remain Muslims, with certain rights that must be respected by an Islamic government. Blasphemers, apostates, on the
other hand, are "corrupt." They are "oppressors" of their own forces
and seek to extend their iniquitous rule to others. They have forfeited
the protections that are the right of Muslims. They are not to be protected; rather, the task of a just government is to eliminate them.

The Iran-Iraq war is thus an example of contemporary conflict in
which classical Islamic thought appears to function well. But other examples are not so clear. Many, if not most, of the situations of conflict
discussed by contemporary Muslims appear to have a somewhat different character. They involve bands of irregulars—"soldiers" who do
not represent an established government and are thus "without portfolio"—in efforts to overthrow regimes that are in one way or another
"non-Islamic" and therefore unjust. The name that Palestinians living
in the West Bank and Gaza gave to their efforts against Israeli occupation during the 1980s is apposite for many of these conflicts: *al-intifada*,
"the shaking off." The goal of such efforts by Muslim irregulars is to
overturn injustice, to establish or reestablish regimes in accord with Islamic values, and thus to carry out the mission of Islam: to struggle for
peace, order, and justice in the earth. In the terms of classical scholars,
this is a type of "defensive jihad."

Classical scholars did not give much consideration to this notion. We have seen that most of them, like al-Shaybani, wrote in a context where Islam was associated with a great imperial establishment. The boundary of the empire—what one might call the "frontier" of Islam— was the place where the jihad to expand Islamic hegemony took place. For classical, especially Sunni, scholars, the norm was offensive war, at the command and by the direction of the caliph. Examples of the type of defensive war that is fought in order to expel an invader making significant progress into Islamic territory were fewer in number and less important.

One of the great exceptions to this generalization is the Crusades. For Muslims, the various invasions of Syria, Palestine, and (what came to be called) Turkey by European Christians during the tenth through the thirteenth century marked a great period of struggle, not only between Muslims and Christians but within the territory of Islam itself. The single greatest hero of the period from the Muslim point of view is Saladin, who from 1169 to 1193 led his armies, first to establish himself as the undisputed leader of the Muslims in Egypt and Syria, then against the Crusaders. Writing that "Islam is now awake to drive away the night phantom of unbelief," Saladin managed in October of 1187 to recover Jerusalem from the European Christians.[21] He celebrated this accomplishment with an observance of Friday prayers at the al-Aqsa mosque.

For some contemporary Islamic groups, the struggle of Saladin with the Crusaders serves as a lens through which to interpret their situation. For example, the group known as Hamas, which styles itself as the specifically *Islamic* wing of the Palestinian movement, argues that the current situation of Palestinians, living under Israeli rule or dispersed from their homeland, is the result of an ongoing crusade by Christians to wrest the Holy Lands from Muslim control. The basic rationale and program for Hamas is set forth in its Charter, where we are told that, after Saladin defeated the Crusaders,

> the Crusaders then knew that it was impossible to defeat the Muslims except by setting the stage with an ideological attack to confuse their (the Muslims') thoughts, stain their heritage and defame their history, after which a military attack would take place.[22]

From other parts of this Charter, one perceives that the "ideological attack" was carried out by nineteenth-century Western scholars and missionaries. The military attack, on the other hand, took place during World War I when European colonialists "liberated" the Holy Lands from the Turks only to assume control themselves. Hamas'

Charter depicts an important sentiment among Muslims when it describes the results:

> (General Edmund) Allenby claimed when he entered Jerusalem *"Now the Crusades are over."* And General Guroud stood by [Saladin's] grave saying, *"Here we have returned O Saladin."*[23]

From the perspective of the Hamas movement, the loss of Palestine (or the creation of Israel as a Jewish State) is an unmeasurable tragedy, not only for Palestinians who have lost homes or land but for the entire Islamic community. The creation of Israel resulted, says the Hamas Charter, from a conspiracy in which the great powers of East and West (i.e., the Soviet Union and the coalition between Great Britain, France, and the United States) collaborated with the aims of Zionists to establish a bridgehead in the territory of Islam. The Zionists

> are behind the first world war where they destroyed the Islamic caliphah and picked the material profit and monopolized on the raw wealth and got the Balfour declaration. And they created the League of Nations so they can control the world through that organization and they are behind the second world war where they grossed huge profits from their trade of war materials and they set down the foundations to establish their nation by forming the United Nations and Security Council ... in order to rule the world through that organization.[24]

It seems strange that Hamas would accuse the Soviet Union and the United States both of working for Zionist goals. Most observers would argue that the differences between the two powers with respect to Israel were, until the dissolution of the Soviet Union, more important than the similarities. For the writers of the Charter, however,

> the imperialist powers in the Capitalist west and the Communist east support the enemy with all their might, material and human, and they change roles. When Islam is manifest the unbelieving powers unite against it because the Nation of the unbelievers is one.[25]

In this context, jihad or struggle in the way of God takes on a special character. It is not the war to expand the territory of Islam envisioned by classical Sunni jurists. Nor is it a war between groups of Muslims, so that the rules relating to rebellion can be operative. Rather, Muslims are said to struggle in the manner of Saladin. Their goal is to rid themselves of the rule of non-Muslims and to recover a lost portion of the territory of Islam. In this sense, the Hamas Charter presents a specifically Islamic rationale for al-intifada—the "shaking off" of illegitimate rule. The purpose of jihad, in this document, is not conquest but recovery—not expansion but restoration.

Granted that Hamas has a rationale for its struggle, a number of issues important in the ethics of war remain. For example: One of the great problems associated with irregular war has to do with the criterion of right authority. For both just war and jihad traditions, the right to authorize war is normally restricted to established governments. Those associated with Hamas do not act on behalf of such a government, however. Indeed, they present themselves as the sworn enemies, not only of the governments of "foreign" countries (e.g., Israel) but of all "so-called" Muslim governments that collaborate with non-Muslim powers (e.g., by negotiating peace treaties with Israel or by allowing the United States and others to place troops in the Arabian peninsula during the Gulf War). For Hamas, Muslim governments who cooperate with the West either do not understand the true intentions of the non-Muslim nations or are corrupt. For anyone with eyes to see, it is plain that

> World Zionism and imperialist powers try with audacious maneuvers and well formulated plans to extract the Arab nations one by one from the struggle with Zionism so in the end it can deal singularly with the Palestinian people. They have already removed Egypt out of the circle of the struggle with the treason of Camp David, and it is trying to extract other countries by using similar treaties. . . . The Islamic Resistance Movement calls upon the Arab and Islamic people to work seriously and constructively in order not to allow that horrible plan to be carried out and to educate the masses of the dangers of withdrawal from the struggle with Zionism. Today it is Palestine and tomorrow it will be another country and then another. The Zionist plan has no bounds and after Palestine they wish to expand from the Nile to the Euphrates.[26]

In their struggle to recover Islamic territory, then, organizations like Hamas cannot look to established governments for authorization. They must find it elsewhere. In essence, their argument is that the Western powers' ideological, military, and political incursions into Islamic territory have created an emergency situation. That being the case, jihad becomes a duty for all conscientious Muslims, and one need not—cannot—wait for authorization other than that given by God: command good and forbid evil. Returning to the classical jurists, we may recall that the ordinary jihad—the struggle to extend the territory of Islam—is a "collective obligation" for the Muslim community. The caliph has the duty to see that enough adult males come forward to carry out the task of expansion. Provided they do, others may stay home or support the effort through giving money and other forms of support. In an extraordinary situation, however—for example, a situation of invasion—jihad is the obligation of each individual Muslim. Everyone must do his—or her—part to restore security to the territory of Islam. Thus the Charter states:

> The Islamic Resistance Movement [firmly] believes that the land of Palestine is an Islamic *Waqaf* [trust] [given to] the Muslim generations till the Day of Resurrection. It is not right to give it up or any part of it. No Arab state, . . . no King or leader, . . . no organization, Palestinian or Arab has such authority. . . .

> There is not a higher peak in nationalism or depth in devotion than: if an enemy lands on the Muslim territories then *Jihad* and fighting the enemy becomes an individual obligation on every Muslim and Muslimah (female Muslim). *The woman is allowed to go fight without the permission of her husband and the slave without the permission of his master.*[27]

In this last line, in particular, one understands the way Hamas wishes to relate the current situation of Muslims to classical Islam. The exceptional situation before the Muslims, in Palestine and in other parts of the world, suspends the usual lines of order between husband and wife, slave and master, government and citizen so that every conscientious Muslim is authorized, in obedience to God, to participate with other believers in the struggle to restore hegemony to Islam. In fact, one must go farther than simple authorization. "When an enemy occupies some of the Muslim lands Jihad becomes obligatory on every Muslim."[28] The Charter itself is thus a call to Muslims to approach the Palestinian cause in the spirit of the following Prophetic *hadith*:

> To guard Muslims from infidels in Allah's cause for one day is better than the world and whatever is on its surface. And a place in paradise as small as that occupied by the whip of one of you is better than the world and whatever is on its surface. And a morning or an evening's journey which the worshiper [undertakes] in Allah's cause is better than the world and what is on its surface.

> By Him in whose Hand is Muhammad's life, I love to be killed in the way of Allah then to be revived to life again, then to be killed and then to be revived to life and then to be killed.[29]

In chapter 4 we noted that much of the current literature on jihad does not deal extensively with the conduct of war. The Hamas Charter is no exception to this, focusing instead on issues connected with the *jus ad bellum*. Part of the struggle, as the document makes clear, is to enliven Muslims to fight. Discussion of tactics seems to be beside the point. Muslims must become a "cooperative society," united against an enemy that uses deception and vicious tactics against them. Nevertheless the claim is made that the "Islamic Resistance Movement is a humanistic movement [that] takes care of human rights and follows the tolerance of Islam with respect to people of other faiths. Never does it attack any of them except those who show enmity towards it or [stand] in its path to stop the movement or waste its efforts."[30] In these terms, Hamas' position is reminiscent of Yassir Arafat's suggestion of the way discrimination plays a part in the PLO's struggle: the fight is with Zionists rather than Jews.[31] On the other hand, the Hamas Charter is not always careful to maintain such distinctions, speaking against Jews in terms that suggest collective guilt, even participation in a battle marking the "end times."

> The Prophet of Allah . . . says: The Last Hour would not come until the Muslims fight against the Jews and the Muslims would kill them, and until the Jews would hide themselves behind a stone or a tree and a stone or a tree would say: Muslim or Servant of Allah there is a Jew behind me; come and kill him; but the tree of Gharqad would not say it, for it is the tree of the Jews.[32]

Ultimately, the Hamas Charter argues, the jihad to liberate Palestine will yield a beneficent and just regime for all people. In the meantime, however, the stark definition of the situation of Muslims and the unity demanded for their struggle do not lend themselves to careful distinctions. Neither does the reality of the means available to the members of Hamas; in the manner of irregular forces throughout history, these must carry on the "fight" with the superior forces of the enemy with whatever tools are at their disposal: economic boycotts; stone throwing; acts of lethal violence by individuals or small groups must be the rule, because the organization cannot risk the type of direct engagement characteristic of public war. The words of a contemporary Islamic jurist ring true here, although they spring from the situation in Lebanon rather than Palestine: "The weak will fight to defend their interests, even if they have to use knives and stones to spread chaos throughout the earth."[33]

The example from Lebanon reminds us that the Palestinians' characterization of their struggle as *al-intifada*, the drive to "shake off" non-Islamic rule, provides a model for understanding many of the conflicts that beset the Islamic world today. Wherever one finds among Muslims organized groups of "soldiers without portfolio," carrying on a fight through irregular or nonconventional tactics, the pattern of reasoning exemplified in the Charter is typical. If we turn, for example, to the text called *The Neglected Duty*, advertised as the "testament" of Islamic Jihad, the Egyptian group famous for the assassination of Anwar Sadat, the same arguments appear.[34]

The Neglected Duty begins with a summons directed at all Muslims. Quoting Qurʾan 57:16, the author speaks thusly:

> Is it not high time for those who have believed to humble their hearts to the Reminder of God and to the truth which He has sent down; and that they should not be like those to whom the Book was formerly given, and for whom the time was long, so that their hearts became hard, and many of them are reprobates?

The author cites traditional sources to indicate that this verse was revealed when "God deemed the hearts of the believers to be slow."[35] As one reads *The Neglected Duty*, it is clear that one purpose of the text is to communicate a sense of urgency. Muslims, we are told, have been and are being victimized. In particular, the territory of Islam is being divided and controlled by non-Muslim powers. There are Muslims who do not see this, and they are ignorant. There are others who, in the name of "modernization," actively cooperate with the unbelievers. These are apostates. *The Neglected Duty* attempts to enliven the former and to provide justification for jihad against the latter.

By way of comparison with the Hamas Charter, one notes the following steps in the argument of *The Neglected Duty*. First, in a section entitled "The Enemy Who Is Near and the Enemy Who Is Far," the authors discuss the relationship of their struggle in Egypt to the efforts of Palestinians. Noting that it "is true that the liberation of the Holy Land is a religious command, obligatory for all Muslims," the author nevertheless states unequivocally that "the first battlefield for jihad is the extermination of . . . infidel leaders and to replace them by a complete Islamic order."[36] First, purify the Muslim community. Then fight to liberate Islamic territory. That is the order of jihad, according to *The Neglected Duty*.

Second, and related to this point, the historical analogy cited by the author is not the Crusades but the fourteenth-century struggle of Muslims with the Mongols. The rationale for this choice is important: from the standpoint of *The Neglected Duty*, the primary enemies of Islam are Muslim traitors—apostates, in particular among those presently in power in Islamic lands. The struggle thus called for is in the first place a struggle between two groups, both of which are ostensibly Islamic. Even so, the discussion of scholars at the time of the Mongol invasion indicates that the "Islamicity" of the Mongols was a crucial issue in determining the propriety of resistance to their rule. Having attended to the classical distinctions related to *ahkam al-bughat*, the "judgments concerning rebels," we can appreciate that *The Neglected Duty* includes a section entitled "Is to Fight Them (the Same as) Fighting the (Group of Rebels Traditionally Called) Al-Bughah?"[37] The answer is that they—whether Mongols or those currently in power in Egypt—are not rebels. They are apostates, so that fighting them is not governed by the limits established by Ali b. Abi Talib. Apostates are no longer Muslims; rather, they are unbelievers. Indeed, they are worse than other unbelievers, since their unbelief has the character of treason. Following the example of Abu Bakr (above), the present rulers should be given fair warning and opportunity to repent. But, failing repentance, they should be killed for the sake of the Muslim community.

These arguments raise the crucial issues connected with irregular war. The author of *The Neglected Duty* advocates, in effect, a mass resistance aimed at overthrowing an established government. As such, Islamic fighters are again in the role of "soldiers without portfolio." What or who authorizes their struggle? And, since the suggestion is that the present rulers of Egypt (and, by implication, other Muslim countries) should be removed from office and killed, what tactics will be used in the course of the jihad? How will the irregulars view the forces of the established government? What of ordinary citizens, Muslims who remain aloof from the struggle? Will the irregulars resort to deception?

A careful reading of *The Neglected Duty* indicates that the author has not only thought about these questions but has a well-developed set of answers. Authorization, for example, is the value at stake in discussions of "Revolt Against the Ruler," "The Establishment of an Islamic State," "The House in Which We Live," "The Ruler Who Rules by Other (Laws) than (the Laws) Which God Sent Down," and "The Rulers of the Muslims Today Are in Apostasy from Islam."[38] Revolution, we are told, is always wrong, except in cases where the caliph "suddenly becomes an unbeliever" through a "public display" of unbelief.[39] The public display can consist in a number of acts, but the most significant from the standpoint of *The Neglected Duty* is that the leader "introduces an innovation."[40] Innovation (*bid^cah*) refers specifically to policies, teachings, or actions that violate the precedents established in the Qur'an or the reports of the Prophet's words and deeds.

Quoting from classical sources, *The Neglected Duty* goes on to say that once a leader

> introduces an innovation . . . he has no longer the qualifications needed in a Leader, to obey him is no longer necessary, and the Muslims have the duty to revolt against him and to depose him, and to put a Just [leader] in his place when they are able to do so. When this occurs to a group of people, they have the duty to revolt and depose the infidel.[41]

Authority, given by God to a Muslim ruler, is thus lost when the ruler commits apostasy. One might say that the Muslims, individually and collectively, are responsible to God for the creation and maintenance of an Islamic state, so that when the ruler forfeits his claim to leadership, political authority devolves to the community as a whole. The question of authorization for irregular forces is thus answered by referring to the rights of God and the responsibilities of Muslims. As if to ensure that readers will be entirely clear on this point, *The Neglected Duty* continues with the explanation that this citation "is also the refutation of those who say that it is only permissible to fight under a Caliph or a Commander."[42] The command is to fight in the name and in the path of God, for the purpose of establishing an Islamic political order. Where those who bear the title of ruler are in effect "no rulers at all," then it becomes "high time for those who have believed" to show obedience to God by revolutionary activity.

The Neglected Duty takes the argument further in "The House in Which We Live."[43] The question under discussion is: Is Egypt an Islamic state? Citing classical precedents, the authors argue that the litmus test that any Islamic state must pass has to do with the nature and sources of its laws. On this matter, Egypt is comparable with most of its neighbors: its constitution and laws are a mix of traditional Islamic judgments, particularly in the area of family law, and European law codes. In the judgment of the authors of *The Neglected Duty*, this means that Egypt is not part of the territory or house of Islam but has become part of the territory of war.

The existence of a mixed legal regime is in fact the "innovation" of which present-day rulers are guilty. *The Neglected Duty* implies that these rulers are also personally corrupt. Nevertheless the imposition of non-Islamic laws on their subjects is the critical factor in the ultimate argument justifying revolutionary activity: that is, that the present rulers of Egypt are apostates. This judgment is stated at considerable length in the text, as follows:

The Rulers of this age are in apostasy from Islam. They were raised at the tables of imperialism, be it Crusaderism, or Communism, or Zionism. They carry nothing from Islam but their names, even though they pray and fast and claim (*idda'a*) to be Muslim.[44]

Quoting the great thirteenth-century jurist Ibn Taymiyya, the authors then note that

it is a well-established rule of Islamic Law that the punishment of an apostate will be heavier than the punishment of someone who is by origin an infidel (and who has never been a Muslim), and this in many respects. For instance, an apostate has to be killed in all circumstances, he does not have the right to profess his new religion against the payment of the head tax, and there can be no Convenant [*sic*] of Protection (between an ex-Muslim and the Muslim authorities) unlike the case with someone who has always been an infidel (non-Muslim, e.g., a Christian or a Jew). . . . Any group of people that rebels against any single prescript of the clear and reliably transmitted prescripts of Islam has to be fought, according to the leading scholars of Islam, even if the members of this group pronounce the Islamic Confession of Faith. If such people make a public formal confession of their (Islamic) Faith (by pronouncing the double formula "There is no god but God, and Muhammad is His Apostle") but, at the same time, refuse to carry out the five daily prayer ceremonies, then it is obligatory to fight them. If they refuse to pay (the religious tax called) *zakat*, it is obligatory to fight them until they pay the *zakat*. Similarly, if they refuse to keep the Fast of the Month of Ramadan or (to perform the Pilgrimage) to the Ancient House (the Ka'bah), and similarly if they refuse to forbid abominations or adultery or gambling or wine or anything else that is forbidden by the laws of Islam. Similarly, if they refuse to apply on matters of life and property, or merchandise and commodities of any kind the Judgment of the Book and the Example (of the Prophet).[45]

The point is abundantly clear. Any Muslim ruler who omits to impose the regimen specified by the traditional judgments of classical jurists as the law of the state is an apostate and must be fought. An army of irregulars, opposing themselves to an established government of this sort, are simply good, conscientious Muslims responding to the claims of God in a situation not of their own making.

What about the means of struggle? Irregulars, as previously noted, often feel justified in using unconventional tactics because of certain realities: the forces of the established government outnumber them and have superior firepower. *The Neglected Duty* notes that this is likely to be the case but does not regard it as unusual. "Muslim armies in the course of the centuries have been small and ill-prepared, encountering armies double their size."[46] The point is reiterated in a number of sections dealing with tactics: The means of war appropriate to Muslims fighting to remove an unjust regime are set, not by considerations of numbers or assessments of the likelihood of victory, but by judgments of the nature of the enemy. The crucial judgment is that the Muslims are *not* fighting a war against rebels but against apostates and infidels. This sets the context for everything else.

Deception, for example, is an acceptable tactic—though there are limits on this judgment. The Muslims must not break treaties or violate explicit promises to enemy personnel. Further, although "lying is essentially permitted," "it is better to limit oneself to speaking ambiguously."[47] As an example, *The Neglected Duty* relates the story of the killing of Ka'b ibn al-Ashraf, a Jew who recited invective poetry against Muhammad and his companions.[48] According to the story, several of Muhammad's associates feigned friendship with al-Ashraf, even to the point of suggesting they agreed with his criticisms of Muhammad. When Ka'b came out with them at night, however, Muhammad's associates took his life. According to *The Neglected Duty*, "In this story are useful lessons in the great art of fighting"—in particular, on the use of deception as a strategy.[49] The goal should be "victory with the fewest losses and by the easiest means possible."[50] Deceptive tactics can include penetration "into the ranks of the infidels"; that is, the use of spies, even if it is probable that the spy will lose his life (that is, the mission might be considered "suicidal").[51] Sections dealing with the prospect of attacking without warning and night raids indicate the permissibility of stealth. In addition, noncombatants or, better, "dependents" of the enemy who are killed as a result of such tactics are victims of their leaders' perfidy, not of any action of the Muslims. As seen in chapter 4, Muslim forces should try to avoid harming such persons but are not responsible for the "indirect" killing that results from actions taken in accord with military necessity.[52]

As also discussed in chapter 4, however, the question of tactics presents different problems when there is a strong possibility that actions taken by the Muslim forces will result in the deaths of Muslims. Prima facie, the struggle envisioned by the author of *The Neglected Duty* raises this problem, since the forces of the established government are largely made up of Muslims. Even if the leaders of the State are considered apostates, those in the army may be Muslims. They may be ignorant of the issues at stake in the struggle, for example, or they may have been forced in some way to serve in the army of the State. How should the Muslim fighters approach these persons?

The answer of *The Neglected Duty* appeals to military necessity and to divine providence as follows. Essentially, there is no way for the (true) Muslims, engaged in a struggle against the forces of the apostate government, to know what is in the hearts of individual combatants. Judgment of the intentions and faithfulness of each person must be left to God. Citing scholars who argue that those die as martyrs, who fight on the enemy side yet nonetheless are true Muslims, the author reasons that

> we [true Muslims] cannot know who are the ones who were forced into the army of the infidels. We cannot differentiate between those who are and those who are not. When we kill them in accordance with the Command of God we are both rewarded and excused. They, however, will be judged according to their intentions. Whoever is forced into an army of infidels is not able to withdraw from fighting. He will be reunited with his fellow Muslims on the Day of Resurrection. So, when such a person is killed for standing by his religion, this is not greater than the killing of someone from the camp of the Muslims.[53]

The killing of Muslims, who are by definition "innocent," is excused if it is indirect (i.e., unintentional) and accomplished in the course of a legitimate military action.

In a published response to the argument of *The Neglected Duty*, the Shaykh al-Azhar indicated his worry that the Islamic Jihad would initiate a new instance of civil strife in the Muslim community.[54] The concerns voiced in the document and the evident zeal of the authors are understandable, said the Shaykh. In a sense, the argument is justified. Yet if all Muslims who have cooperated in the building of modern Egypt—a state that the author of *The Neglected Duty* describes as "not Islamic"—are potentially apostates and deserve to die, where will the killing stop? Recalling the example of the Kharijites and their (misguided) attempts to purify the Muslim community in the days of Ali, the Shaykh argues that reformers do better to show restraint. In the long run, the formation of an Islamic society is better served by patience and persuasion than by the use of force. A group like Islamic Jihad that acts on the argument of *The Neglected Duty* may even find itself charged with injustice, should its activities bring harm to people regarded by ordinary Muslims as innocent. The militant members of such a group can never constitute a regular army, argued the Shaykh. Their jihad is not authorized by any recognized political authority. And so in the end, the zealots violate Islamic precepts, bringing upon themselves the Qur'anic judgment they would have imposed on others:

> The reward of those who make war upon Allah and His messenger and strive after corruption in the land will be that they will be killed.   (5:33)

With this argument, the Shaykh raises once again the problems of the authorization and conduct of soldiers without portfolio. The struggle envisioned by the author of *The Neglected Duty*, according to the Shaykh, is not a regular jihad.

The author is not without an answer, however. In the manner of irregulars in all times and places, the appeal is that extraordinary circumstances call for unusual approaches. Thus the author argues that fighting "is now a duty upon all Muslims."[55] The situation of the Muslims is such that jihad (in the sense of fighting) is now an "individual duty."[56] Recalling that in classical jurisprudence the jihad to extend Islamic territory (the regular jihad) was a "collective duty" fulfilled so long as the caliph could summon enough eligible men to fight, one understands that *The Neglected Duty* is saying that the current situation of Muslims is irregular. It is so because the recognized political authorities are not legitimate rulers. That being the case, the ordinary restriction of fighting to soldiers serving in a regular army does not apply. One may go farther: Given their current context, individual Muslims are not only permitted to take up arms. They are obligated to do so. For

> with regard to the lands of Islam, the enemy lives right in the middle of them. The enemy even has got hold of the reins of power, for this enemy is (none other than) these rulers who have (illegally) seized the Leadership of the Muslims. Therefore, waging *jihad* against them is an individual duty, in addition to the fact that Islamic *jihad* today requires a drop of sweat from every Muslim.

> Know that when *jihad* is an individual duty, there is no (need to) ask permission of (your) parents to leave to wage *jihad*, as the jurists have said; it is thus similar to prayer and fasting.[57]

Conclusion

From the perspective of groups like Hamas and Islamic Jihad, irregular war is a fact of life. The necessity to struggle against injustice is an obligation that Muslims cannot ignore. That is so whether injustice is manifest through the actions of unbelievers who occupy portions of the Islamic homeland or through rulers who pretend to be good Muslims. The procedural requirements for jihad—for example, that it be conducted only at the behest of an established political authority—cannot be applied in the traditional manner. Ultimately, even the established authority's right to conduct war comes from God. In an extreme situation, God assigns this right to ordinary Muslims. That at least is the argument of the Charter of Hamas and of *The Neglected Duty*. To say that children do not need permission of their parents to fight (*The Neglected Duty*) or that women may participate in the jihad without the permission of their husbands (Charter) is to assume an extreme situation. One could say that the *jus ad bellum* criteria have not been overridden, but they have been transformed by events. Similarly, *jus in bello* requirements like discrimination and proportionality are not overridden in the Hamas Charter or *The Neglected Duty*, but the peculiar type of conflict in which Hamas or Islamic Jihad find themselves involved creates situations in which traditional applications of these notions must be stretched. Assassinations, deception, kidnappings—these are acts which are either justified or excused by the realities of the struggle that contemporary Muslims are commanded to undertake. Or so irregulars argue.

When Francis Lieber wrote the line quoted at the outset of this discussion, and expressed his fears about irregular war, he knew whereof he spoke. Yet his metaphor was inept. Irregulars, at least in the case of contemporary Islam, do not lay the ax to their moral traditions. Rather, the danger of war conducted by irregulars is that they, perceiving themselves as warriors who are beleaguered yet just, will stretch the fragile fabric of religious and moral traditions on the limitation of war so far that it breaks. Contemporary Muslim irregulars do not set out to overturn their tradition. But finding that their tradition provides them with many notions that do not correspond to the realities they perceive, they risk stretching the tradition farther than it will bear. Classical Islam was not without an understanding of the issues connected with irregular war. Indeed, the reasoning of the jurists on the judgments pertaining to rebels presents a fascinating case of premodern reflection on this phenomenon. As a guide to modern conflicts, though, the tradition does not always provide useful precedents. The "fit" between past and present is not precise.

One conclusion of this discussion must therefore be to emphasize (as in chapter 4) the changed context in which Muslims now develop their traditions on the justification and limitation of war. Those who live and struggle in the twentieth century confront a very different social and political reality than did their premodern ancestors. There is no imperial state, no caliph; in one sense, no clearly defined territory that Muslims can claim as "Islamic." New forms of political discourse and organization, and new legal institutions, have found their way into the lives of Muslims. With this in mind, some writers suggest that we live in a period of "Islamic Reformation," in which the values and symbols of premodern understandings of the tradition conflict with new and emerging ways to order and understand life.

The difficulty with the analogy lies in the source from which ideas of reform flow. Whatever else it was, Europe's Reformation was an "internal" affair. Roman Catholics and Protestants of various stripes all read the Bible. All shared a certain set of religious and moral symbols. And no party could criticize its opponents as "tools of the foreigners," in the sense of working with parties outside Christian culture.

Contemporary Muslims live in a different context. Their politicians and religious leaders must always live with the possibility that the opposition will be able to portray them as importers of foreign ideas. As the arguments of the Hamas Charter and of *The Neglected Duty* show, one way to express opposition to established political arrangements in the traditionally Islamic countries is to speak about a conspiracy on the part of infidels, outsiders to the region and its values; a conspiracy that succeeds in part because Muslim leaders are corrupt and the Muslim people are unaware.

How should Westerners respond to this phenomenon? One school of thought holds that Europeans, Americans, and their leaders ought to listen to the anger expressed by militant groups. The way to peace is through dialogue, and the first step is to recognize that Muslims who act in ways that cause pain to Western interests are responding to a pain of their own. In particular, one should be careful not to think in terms of an implacable Islam uncompromisingly hostile to Western ideas and interests. Militant groups do not speak for all Islam; they are a particular manifestation of Islamic sentiment in the light of special circumstances. If Europeans and Americans will listen, they will understand that the concerns for justice, human rights, and self-determination that such groups reflect are legitimate, even if their methods are excessive.

Such at least is the argument of Shaykh Muhammad Hussein Fadlallah, spiritual leader of the Party of God (Hizbullah), a militant or irregular group generally held responsible for kidnappings and terror activities in Lebanon throughout the 1980s. In an interview published in 1986, the Shaykh appealed to the American people to develop a more subtle understanding of the relationship of Islam to the actions of militant groups. As he put it,

> We do not hold in our Islamic belief that violence is the solution to
> all types of problems; rather, we see violence as a kind of surgical

operation that a person should use only after trying all other means, and only when he finds his life imperiled.[58]

Here Shaykh Fadlallah speaks the traditional language of Islam, particularly of Shiism, in arguing that violence is justified only for defensive purposes and as a last resort. The contemporary outbreak of violence in the Middle East, he tells us, must be understood in terms of the recent history of the region. In particular, violence by Muslim "irregulars"

> emanates from given political, economic and social conditions which have been imposed on reality by a great oppressive power that has intruded in pursuit of its economic and strategic interests. The violence began as the people, feeling themselves bound by impotence, stirred to shatter some of that enveloping powerlessness for the sake of liberty.[59]

The situation imposed upon the people of the Middle East, in particular upon Muslims, by the establishment of Israel, the dislocation of Palestinians, and the continuing interference of the United States in Arab-Islamic affairs brings about a situation that breeds violence. To put it another way, Shaykh Fadlallah wants us to consider that recent history creates a context in which some Muslims (read: groups of irregulars) consider themselves justified in using force to achieve their ends. Further, the situation is such that people who resort to force sometimes engage in behavior that is extreme. Thus Shaykh Fadlallah considers that

> kidnapping people is not excused from a Muslim point of view. In Islam, the Qur'an says, "Do not burden yourself by adding another's to your own," meaning that no person should carry the weight of someone else's crimes. That is why I declare from a responsible, rather than from a defensive position that I am against all kidnappings, and that I do not see any righteousness in any acts of kidnapping, be they of Frenchmen or Americans, of airliners or ships. I might sympathize with the cause of the hijackers, but I do not endorse the means they use, because I believe that the Americans they are seizing are participants in cultural, medical, and social institutions, and cannot be held responsible for the actions of their governments.[60]

Here, the Shaykh suggests that irregulars have gone too far in the conduct of their struggle. More traditional notions of discrimination, based on an understanding of degrees of guilt, should be observed by Muslims struggling for their rights.

Nevertheless the onus for improving the situation is clearly on the United States and its allies. Thus Shaykh Fadlallah concluded his interview with a call to the American people to press for reforms in the government's policies. If the present situation does not change, he argued, there will be a world war of terrorism, in which the "weak will fight to defend their interests, even if they have to use knives and stones to spread chaos throughout the earth."[61]

Americans and Europeans certainly should be able to understand Shaykh Fadlallah's logic. And those who value the liberty achieved by bands of irregulars in, for example, the American Revolution can hardly miss the reflection of notions that in extreme circumstances a people is justified in rising up against a government it considers illegitimate. No doubt, to listen to Shaykh Fadlallah and other spokespersons with care increases one's understanding of those Muslims who resort to force and of Muslim perceptions of current political arrangements in general. No doubt, Europeans and Americans can go some distance toward "addressing the underlying problems of the Middle East," as people sometimes say.

But listening, understanding, and accommodating are distinct activities. To understand some of the difficulties involved in addressing the underlying problems of the region, let us examine one very visible attempt to express concerns for justice in the traditionally Islamic countries. As the Gulf Crisis built toward war in the fall of 1990, and again in the months following the Allied victory, President George Bush spoke of his vision of a New World Order—a vision with roots not only in the President's mind but in the U.N. Charter, in post-World War II notions of collective security, and, in a sense, in the religious and cultural traditions of the West and Islam. Theoretically, the President's vision rested on notions of the self-determination of peoples, respect for human rights, and concerns for justice. All these are things associated with "addressing the underlying problems in the Middle East." How did President Bush's vision square with religious and political realities in the Middle East? What are the chances for a constructive engagement between Euro-American and Muslim interests, as we move beyond the Gulf War?

CHAPTER SIX

Religion and World Order

To raise questions like those with which chapter 5 ends seems at first to exceed the limits of a study of ethics. Such questions are political: they do not bear directly on an analysis of either just war tradition or the rules for jihad; neither can answers to such questions be straightforwardly derived from analyses of noncombatant immunity or irregular war.

At the same time, our discussions have made clear that just war and jihad traditions are by their nature related to issues of political order. The rules for jihad fit into the context of the Islamic community's sense of mission; they play a part in that community's attempt to build a world in which peace, order, and justice prevail according to the providence of God. Similarly, just war tradition is one aspect of a theory of statecraft in which human beings preserve the relative balance of peace, order, and justice available to them in this world. That the just war tradition or the rules for jihad can be described, as in these pages, as the military portion of a cultural tradition reflecting specific views of the nature and purposes of human society makes it difficult, if not impossible, to avoid political questions in discussing them. That would be so, even if our inquiry did not take place in the context in which it does: a context in which the traditions we call "Western" and "Islamic" are bumping into one another each and every day.

When George Bush said that the Gulf War presented an opportunity to build a "new world order," then, he spoke of an idea that has real import for this study. Readers will recall that in October 1990, as Iraq on one side and the United States and its allies on the other confronted one another in the Persian Gulf, Mr. Bush gave a speech at the United

Nations. The end of the Cold War, said the President, brought with it the opportunity to build a new world order. The Gulf Crisis (and eventually, war) would be a first test of our resolve to move in that direction.

The President went on to describe what the new order might be. Its key task "now, first, and always," as he put it, would "be to demonstrate that aggression will not be tolerated."[1] In particular, Mr. Bush argued that the nations of the world had an immediate opportunity to serve the cause of international order by responding firmly to the aggression perpetrated by Iraq against Kuwait.

In giving collective security pride of place, the President said nothing new. The U.N. Charter similarly speaks of cooperation against aggression as the keystone of international order. The President went on to voice his hopes that other aspirations expressed in that Charter might also be fulfilled as a result of the new political context. Provided it stood firm against Iraq, the international community might benefit from new security arrangements, guaranteed by improved cooperation among the great powers at the United Nations. Such arrangements might bring about the elimination of chemical and biological weapons. More than this, Mr. Bush saw humanity moving toward the formation of a "world of open borders, open trade, and, most importantly, open minds . . . taking pride not just in hometown or homeland but in humanity itself." Especially in the Middle East, there would be "opportunities for Iraq and Kuwait to settle their differences permanently, for the states of the gulf themselves to build new arrangements for stability and for all the states and peoples of the region to settle the conflicts that divide the Arabs from Israel."[2] Following the war, President Bush reiterated these goals: a new world order will be built, he said, on the foundations of international resolve to seek "[p]eaceful settlements of disputes, solidarity against aggression, reduced and controlled arsenals, and just treatment of all peoples."[3]

The nations of the world did stand firm, and Iraq was forcibly driven from Kuwait. With joint sponsorship from the United States and the (soon to be defunct) Soviet Union, Arabs and Israelis began a series of unprecedented negotiations. The collapse of the Soviet Union led to agreements between the United States and the new Commonwealth of Independent States that will, if fulfilled, drastically reduce numbers of nuclear warheads.

But people stopped talking about the New World Order. What happened?

Many had been skeptical about the notion from the start. A. M. Rosenthal, for example, devoted a number of columns in the *New York Times* to exposing moral inconsistencies in the Bush Administration's policies. The day after the president's address at the United Nations, Rosenthal's column bore the title "Our Ally, the Killer." The article noted the similarities between Saddam Hussein and Syrian leader Hafez al-Assad and asked whether it was appropriate to taint our efforts against the former by increasing our cooperation with the latter. Rosenthal expanded his criticism in later columns; when the Soviet Union sent troops into Lithuania in late December of 1990, his column began with the observation that the new world order, supposedly begun with the advent of international sanctions against Iraq in August, had been extremely short-lived. It died, according to Rosenthal, when the world did nothing to stop the Soviet army. For Rosenthal, the international focus on Saddam Hussein served mainly to provide a cover for other tyrants to carry out their own programs of terror and abuse. The New World Order was simply rhetoric for wartime consumption.

Of course, the Bush Administration could have objected (if it had cared to) that the New World Order was not an accomplished task. It was an agenda—something to strive for, a goal to accomplish. But other critics, with deeper suspicions than Rosenthal's, would have seen even that response as troublesome. A September 1990 issue of the *Crescent International*, a pro-Iranian newspaper printed in Toronto, responded to the international coalition against Iraq with the headline: "U.S. inaugurates a new age of colonialism by a single power."[4] As the writer saw it, the only thing new about the New World Order was that there was no great power to balance out the United States. The same newspaper would later carry an editorial featuring a similar analysis of the Arab-Israeli peace talks.[5] Here, the writer observed, we see the newfound power of the United States: talks over the fate of Palestine that feature a joint Jordanian-Palestinian delegation led by Christians and secularists. Why no Muslims in the delegation? Because the negotiations are organized to do the will of the United States, which is solidly against Islam. For all the appearance of a new international solidarity, the *Crescent* argued, the post–Cold War, post–Gulf War world was in fact unipolar and the United States was calling the shots.

With respect to U.S. discussion of the New World Order, one supposes that the most important reasons for the lack of continuing interest had to do with President Bush's internal political problems. Between the summer of 1991 and the summer of 1992, the president's popularity dropped steadily. Polls indicated a general feeling that the Bush Administration spent too much time on foreign policy and had little to say about domestic affairs. In such an atmosphere, further attempts to define and advance new international arrangements simply lacked appeal.

At a more substantive level, however, the Bush proposal was stymied by numerous ethnic conflicts. Iraq's repression of Kurdish and Shiite rebellions and the recurrence of old religious and ethnic conflicts that had been controlled by "nations" like Yugoslavia or the Soviet Union made some people long for the "peace of a sort" characteristic of the "old order." In such a context, the utopian tendencies present in President Bush's rhetoric begged for an exchange like the one recounted in Boswell's *Life of Johnson*:[6]

> BOSWELL: So, Sir, you laugh at schemes of political improvement.
>
> JOHNSON: Why, Sir, most schemes of political improvement are very laughable things.

Even President Bush took aim at those whose hopes might have been too high. In sharp contrast to Francis Fukayama's essay "The End of History," the president's line in various presentations was: This is the time of "reemergent history." For peoples like the Serbs and the Croats, or the Armenians and the Azerbaijanis (not to mention the Kurds), the Cold War "order" had been a time of stagnation. Now, post–Cold War, post–Gulf War, such peoples felt free once more to pursue their traditional visions of peace, order, and justice. And conflict was a natural, though unfortunate effect of such freedom.

The notion of "reemergent history" points squarely to issues for which the current study is relevant. Islam, as other religious and cultural traditions, carries its own vision—really, visions of world order. When Saddam Hussein and other Iraqi leaders spoke of the Gulf War, they invoked one interpretation of that vision:

> Honorable Arabs, true Muslim believers, freedom-loving people around the world. Ever since the United States, Zionism, and the United States' imperialist Western Allies came to realize that an Arab Muslim country, Iraq, was developing a force of its own, capable of being a counterweight to the imperialist-backed Zionism—a free, honorable, force, resolved selflessly to tackle Zionist aggression and greed, and to reject imperialist hegemony over the region—the United States, Zionism, and all colonial powers who entertained hatred against Arabs and Muslims set about taking measures, making decisions, and waging campaigns of falsehoods and incitement against Iraq, with the object of thwarting the creation and development of this force, and isolating and punishing Iraq, because it has faithfully, determinedly, and efficiently gone beyond the limits set by the United States, imperialism, and imperialist forces for the states of the region.

The statement, issued by the Iraqi Revolutionary Command Council as a "peace proposal" on February 15, 1990 (one month into Operation Desert Storm), went on to say that the invasion of Kuwait was "not as portrayed by the U.S. and colonialist propaganda. . . . These events were a national, pan-Arab, and Islamic uprising . . . against injustice, immorality, corruption, and imperialist-Zionist-colonialist hegemony of the region."[7]

One of the questions posed in the introduction to this study had to do with the legitimacy of Iraq's characterization of its confrontation with the West as a jihad. The answer, it seems, is that Iraq's use of jihad terminology, while not legitimate in terms of the full range of classical Islamic thought, nevertheless represents one way that such terminology can be developed. In the context of twentieth-century politics, Saddam Hussein's adaptation of the symbolic (though not the legal-ethical) dimensions of jihad in terms of the struggle for Arab-Islamic rights to territory and self-determination has a certain plausibility. And it is interesting, given President Bush's description of ours as a time of "reemergent history," that some argued that Iraq might never have attempted to expand its territory had the Cold War order still held in August of 1990. In that order, Iraq could have status as a client of the Soviet Union (and, during the war with Iran, of the United States as well). Post–Cold War, however, Iraq felt it had the opportunity to pursue a historic agenda—to lead the Arab, Muslim people to their rightful place on the world stage.

We have also seen, however, that Islam sustains visions of world order far more broad and deep than that articulated by Saddam Hussein. In the pragmatic idealism of classical Sunni theorists; in the attempt of Shiite intellectuals to sustain yet restrict political authority in the light of their eschatological hopes; in the struggles of contemporary groups of Muslim "irregulars" to honor yet stretch the tradition that they have inherited, we have seen the power of one religious and cultural tradition to motivate and organize not only political action but intellect. In that sense, one point of the various chapters that make up this book might be to reinforce a judgment made in chapter 1—the "Islamic resurgence" characteristic of our time cannot be explained as simple nostalgia (as some have argued), or even as the result of outrage at injustice (as others claim). It flows from the sense of mission that has always been a part of Islam. The imperative to command good and forbid evil, or to build a just social order on earth, forms a basis for the action and thought of a variety of contemporary Muslim groups. Such groups develop their teaching on force—the military aspect of the Islamic "politico-military doctrine"—in connection with that imperative.

What does this imply for the future of world order? The most obvious answer is rather pessimistic: those who would seek a New World Order in which people take "pride not just in hometown or homeland but in humanity itself" set themselves a very difficult task.

History, we might say, shows its cunning in bringing about the follow-ing irony: the ways in which Western and Islamic cultures understand their current context hinders their ability to accommodate each other's religious and political interests, precisely at a time when technology, economics, and environmental concern make it impossible for them to avoid one another.

Richard Rubenstein, among others, reminds us that religious and cultural traditions express themselves in narratives that foster the "group feeling" of particular communities.[8] Such narratives tie the tra-ditions to specific social and historical experiences. The members of communities are then identified by their ability to say of such experi-ences: That happened to us.

Rubenstein's work focuses on the example of the Holocaust—an event that, whatever else it may be, constitutes a crucial moment in the narrative that shapes the identity of late-twentieth-century Jews. Con-fronted with the destruction wrought by national socialism from 1933 to 1945, Jews say: That happened to us. And the lesson, so often stated by Israel's recent leaders, is that Jews will never let such a slaughter occur again. Even if one takes it, as many Jews do, that the application of this lesson requires protecting all human beings (and not only Jews) from oppression, the narrative serves first to foster communal identity. History reinforces particularity, or the sense of hometown or home-land, rather than of a common humanity.

Even so for some Muslims. In December of 1990, the *New York Times* printed an op-ed essay by the Jordanian writer Rami Khouri.[9] Entitled "The Arab Dream Won't Be Denied," Khouri's essay mingled notions of Arab and Islamic solidarity in much the same manner as the speeches of Saddam Hussein. Recounting the recent history of the Middle East, Khouri argued that "the Arab world has been character-ized [in modern times] by rising frustration with the inability to give expression to grassroots sentiments for a single, pan-Arab national en-tity." This frustration, he said, will eventually lead to a united resis-tance against the West and to the restoration of Arab and Muslim pride. As Khouri put it: "We will not be the world's last colonies." The historical experience of Arabs and Muslims, one might say, yields a narrative of struggle and hope. Remembering the career of Muham-mad, the greatness of the High Caliphate, the struggles with colonial regimes in the nineteenth and early twentieth centuries, and the loss of Palestine, Arabs and Muslims say: That happened to us. And the les-son, articulated by charismatic leaders of every stripe, is this: Muslims have an ongoing mission in the world. We must awaken to our real context, and struggle to fulfill our calling. For "God never changes the condition of a people until they change themselves" (Qur'an 13:11).

Much of the contemporary return to Islam is driven by the perception of Muslims as a community formed by a particular narrative and having a mission to fulfill. That this perception sometimes leads to conflict is not surprising. In encounters between the West and Islam, the struggle is over who will provide the primary definition to world order. Will it be the West, with its notions of territorial boundaries, market economics, private religiosity, and the priority of individual rights? Or will it be Islam, with its emphasis on the universal mission of a transtribal community called to build a social order founded on the pure monotheism natural to humanity? The question for those who envision world order, then, is, "Who determines the shape of order, in the new international context?" The very question suggests a competition between cultural traditions with distinctive notions of peace, order, and justice. It thus implies pessimism concerning the call for a new world order based on notions of common humanity.

But of course that is not the whole picture. Consider for a moment more the question, Who determines the shape of international order? We might also ask, Who determines the shape of particular religious and cultural traditions? Which of the various persons and groups claiming to represent the West or Islam will determine the contemporary form of these traditions? Who will provide the most convincing applications, for example, of the narrative of struggle and hope told by contemporary Muslims? Saddam Hussein? Those inheriting the mantle of the Ayatullah Khumayni? Someone else, as yet unknown?

The point is that diversity exists not only between traditions but within them. In some ways, recognition of this point increases pessimism when one thinks about world order: If one wants to find commonality between the West and Islam, where can one look? Which interpretation is authoritative? Who speaks for the tradition, in either case?

From another perspective, diversity within traditions can be grounds for hope. If traditions are not univocal, it may be that conversation partners can be found, and bridges be built, even between cultural traditions existing in such a difficult position as the West and Islam. History has lent to these traditions a hope that unites and divides: the aspiration to balance peace, order, and justice in a universal civilization—but with a Western or an Islamic "twist." If we can discover ways of understanding that "twist" that suggest commonality, *then* what will we say about the prospects for world order?

Such a project takes on special significance when we consider that the traditions we call "Western" and "Islamic" can no longer strictly be identified with particular geographic regions—despite the current custom of speaking about "the Islamic world" or of identifying

"Western culture" with Europe and North America. The rapidity of Muslim immigration, and the phenomenon of conversions to Islam (particularly in North America), suggest that we may soon be forced to speak not simply of Islam *and*, but of Islam *in*, the West. What difference will this make?

In some cases, Muslims emigrating to Europe or North America have adopted the convention of separation: Islamic communities form a sort of sectarian enclave in the context of a larger, Western culture. In the West but not of it, such communities often advance vigorous criticisms of developments in their new homelands, while enjoying the economic and political benefits offered therein. They are in one sense institutional enactments of the "guest worker" role played by individual Muslims in some European countries. These communities have a certain permanence within the larger culture that the individual guest worker lacks; nevertheless their ability to sustain a separate life-style relies, as does the guest worker's permit, on a certain degree of tolerance from the larger community.

In other cases, Muslim immigrants have taken on an apologetic role. Desirous of acceptance from a culture in which they work, and hoping to enjoy the rights promised to all citizens, such persons often try to distance themselves, and the tradition they love, from association with the political behaviors that Europeans and Americans find distasteful. Alternatively, they offer a rationale for such behaviors that focuses on excusing conditions: the harshness of the political culture of the Middle East, difficult economic conditions, a lack of understanding of the true nature of politics: these are the reasons for hostage taking and other forms of "terrorist" activity. Such actions have nothing to do with true Islam, which is a religion based on peace and the toleration of diverse religious and moral viewpoints.

Other alternatives are available to Muslims who emigrate to the West, to be sure; and many may find both the sectarian and the apologetic role comfortable, depending on their context. The point I wish to advance is this: Muslims in the West will not be cast in these roles forever. They cannot play such roles for long, and be faithful to their tradition; I would also say they should not be so cast. Muslims *will not* play such parts forever, because the usual patterns of economic and educational progress among immigrant groups will lead members of the Islamic community to participate more fully in their new homelands than either the sectarian or the apologetic model allows. Muslims *cannot* permanently be cast in such roles, because the Islamic tradition lends itself to—I would argue, impels—political action. Muslims *should not* be limited to sectarian or apologetic roles, because they offer a perspective that, understood rightly, belongs to a conversation about the nature and direction of human existence that began in ancient Israel and made its way through the long history of the development of Western civilization. With special reference to the current study, the Islamic tradition offers ways of thinking about ethics and the use of force that complement and can extend the cultural tradition of the West as it relates to these matters.

One example will suffice to illustrate both the contemporary problems of Muslims in the West and their potential contribution to discussions of ethics and war. In April of 1992, the United States Institute of Peace (USIP) sponsored a forum titled "Religious Perspectives on the Use of Force After the Gulf War."[10] USIP, a nonprofit institution supported solely by government funding, invited scholars and religious leaders to reflect on the Gulf War from the perspective of three traditions: Judaism, Christianity, and Islam. That much of the discussion centered on the relation of the just war tradition to the Gulf War is understandable. It is that tradition, after all, which has the deepest roots in Western culture; Christian participants in particular had a stake in questions like, "Did the Gulf War satisfy the requirements of the just war tradition?" or, "What did the Bush Administration's appropriation of the just war criteria show about the tradition's usefulness in limiting war?" After all, Christians have been the most visible religious participants in the contemporary revival of interest in the *jus ad bellum* and *jus in bello*. And the U.S. bishops of the Roman Catholic Church arguably did more to educate the public in just war reasoning than did any other group on the contemporary scene when they published their 1983 pastoral *The Challenge of Peace*—thereby cementing the perception that the just war tradition is a Christian invention.

Professor David Novak, however, argued that the just war criteria can also be found in Jewish tradition.[11] While the historic experience of Jews has generally not involved the exercise of political power, and the development of a Judaic perspective on war has therefore suffered, Novak proceeded to draw on Hebrew Scriptures, Talmudic discourses, and law codes to sketch the outlines of a Judaic version of the just war tradition. The assumption of a common vocabulary, or at least the potential for one, allowed for a lively exchange on the possibilities for a distinctive Judaic contribution to judgments about war. Some respondents, for example, argued that a Judaic perspective on justice and war would require more precision than usual with respect to the power to authorize war. Others argued that Judaic sources provided no convenient parallel to the Christian concern that war be a last resort. And some cited further sources in support of the opinion that a Judaic just war tradition would provide a more explicit warrant for environmental concern than is the case in Christian discourse.

The case for some of the respondents' points seemed weak to this observer. But the potential of such an exchange for the identification of commonality and the extension of the just war tradition was clear. One way of understanding Novak's presentation is as follows: Jews and Christians have a shared interest in certain questions concerning the use of force. What are the ends that justify military action? Who decides when those ends are truly at stake? And what are the appropriate military means for pursuing those ends? While Jews and Christians address these questions out of distinctive historical experiences, make use of different sources in their arguments, and reason in ways that indicate these particularities, they can nevertheless understand and benefit from one another. At the least, such an exchange sharpens the thinking of members of each community; at most, there is the possibility of a new, more extensive (and thereby inclusive) tradition on justice and war. In the increasingly pluralistic context of Western culture, it is incumbent on representatives of the Jewish and Christian communities to listen to, argue with, and thereby demonstrate respect for one another.

When it came to perspectives from Islam, the story was slightly different and, to my way of thinking, said as much about the position of Muslims in Western culture as about the justice of the Gulf War. Professor M. M. Ali argued that, since the primary participants in the Gulf War were not motivated by Islam, it was impossible to apply norms developed in the Islamic tradition to this conflict. Other Muslim participants argued similarly that the Gulf War had nothing to do with Islam, and resonated with Ali's comment: "When Kuwait gets attacked, I get hurt. When Iraq gets attacked, I get hurt."[12]

The argument that Islam had nothing to do with the Gulf War is understandable, though from my point of view it must be qualified, as readers know by now. Even more, such an argument is understandable on the part of Muslims in the West, since the social consequences for anyone identified with Iraq during the war could be quite high: Arabs and Muslims in the United States felt their security, and in some cases their lives, to be endangered by the patriotic fervor of their neighbors. To distinguish Islam from Saddam Hussein was a socially desirable as well as an intellectually defensible course to take.

One could not help feeling, however, that Ali was missing an opportunity to educate his listeners. In view of the long experience of Muslims with power, and also of the importance of the historical narrative in which contemporary Islamic discussions of armed struggle make sense, there was much to say for a distinctively Islamic contribution to the USIP forum. Here was an audience, ready and willing to learn of the ways Muslims have developed to adjudicate questions of the justice of war. In one sense, the entire forum could be seen less as a discussion about the Gulf War per se than as a reflection on the variety of ways Jews, Christians, and Muslims suggest we ought to reflect on ethics and the use of force—in the Gulf War or in any other circumstance.

In my response to Ali, I suggested three possibilities for those drawing on the Islamic tradition to think about the Gulf War. First, a Muslim might follow the example of Novak in detailing an Islamic version of the just war criteria. To talk about just cause, last resort, right authority, and the like in distinctively Islamic terms would certainly be a fruitful endeavor and would allow, among other things, a debate over the different ways Muslims and just war thinkers have attempted to implement their concerns to discriminate between the innocent and the guilty in war. That such a debate has considerable potential is indicated, I hope, by the discussion in chapter 4 of this book.

Second, a Muslim might play on the distinction between jihad, as a war legitimated by and fought in a manner consonant with religious values, and *harb*, a war fought for "secular" concerns (oil, political power) and limited for the most part by considerations of political prudence. As indicated in chapter 3, this line of thinking would tap some of the deepest wellsprings of classical and contemporary Islamic thought and has the potential to set the discussion of ethics and war in the wider context of a debate over the place of religion in human society. In connection with the Gulf War, one might proceed to argue that the secular motivations of the major participants classify the war as *harb* and that therefore it is not surprising if they exceeded the limits of acceptable behavior in the conduct of war (e.g., by excessive bombing or damaging the environment).

Third, a distinctively Islamic contribution might try to analyze the Gulf War in terms of *ahkam al-bughat*, or more generally of Islamic perspectives on irregular war. The former in particular would allow attention to the special problems posed for Islamic thought by a war in which Muslims fight one another. As indicated in chapter 5, however, the discussion of irregular war also provides an opportunity to discuss Islamic perceptions of history and of the current distribution of power in the international community. In short, this possibility would have opened the forum to an evaluation of the political realities behind Saddam Hussein's description of his efforts as jihad against imperialism—in effect, a defensive activity.

Again, the point of such an exchange would not necessarily be to find agreement on the Gulf War or on questions of ethics and force in general. It would, however, have allowed participants in the USIP forum to begin to associate Muslims, as well as Jews and Christians, with a certain set of interests in the use of force: for example, that military might be used for morally acceptable goals and that the means of war be limited by similarly acceptable considerations. Such an exchange would also have furthered the sense that Judaism, Christianity, and Islam can develop a vocabulary useful for debating the relationship of these interests to particular instances of armed conflict. Finally, it would have created the opportunity for an identification of the particular resources and perspectives that Muslims, as well as Jews and Christians, bring to the discussion of ethics and war—at the least sharpening those special perspectives, and at the most allowing for a kind of cross-fertilization between the three great monotheistic traditions.

In the introduction to this volume, I cite James Turner Johnson to the effect that the current task facing advocates of the just war tradition is to turn the theoretical universality of that tradition into a practical one, particularly by incorporating non–European, non–North American perspectives. I have some sympathy for that notion; while I think we are a long way from a truly international "just war tradition," and that attaining such a goal will require sifting through the many layers of cultural traditions like Islam, the idea is noble and perhaps, from certain perspectives, a religious or moral imperative. The same might be said for notions of a new world order—it will be a long time coming, if it ever appears; nevertheless there is probably good reason to strive for it. My immediate goal is much smaller, however, and I can put it this way: To learn, through careful study, the wisdom of a tradition that, through force of intellect and long experience with power, has crafted a working doctrine on the relationship between ethics, war, and statecraft. That this tradition is not my own matters little; that I do not always agree with its judgments matters less. From my perspective, to study Islam, as to study ethics, is a way to acknowledge the admonition of Proverbs 4:5: "Get wisdom; get insight." There follows a promise: Wisdom will "keep" those who seek it. May it be so.

Notes

Introduction

1. For an example of James Turner Johnson's work, see, among his other writings, *Just War Tradition and the Restraint of War* (Princeton: Princeton University Press, 1981).

2. There have been some recent attempts, however. See, e.g., the essays collected in the following two volumes: James Turner Johnson and John Kelsay, eds., *Cross, Crescent, and Sword: The Justification and Limitation of War in Western and Islamic Tradition* (Westport, Conn.: Greenwood Press, 1990); and John Kelsay and James Turner Johnson, eds., *Just War and Jihad: Historical and Theoretical Perspectives on War and Peace in Western and Islamic Tradition* (Westport, Conn.: Greenwood Press, 1991).

3. I shall not attempt a theoretical justification of this method here but hope to do so in future publications.

4. Advanced in "Historical Roots and Sources of the Just War Tradition in Western Culture," in Kelsay and Johnson, *Just War and Jihad*, p. 26.

5. Publication information on the two volumes is given in n. 2 above.

Chapter One

1. As published in the *New York Times*, August 11, 1990, A6.

2. Fouad Ajami, *Arab Predicament: Arab Political Thought and Practice Since 1967* (Cambridge: Cambridge University Press, 1981).

3. It is particularly interesting to think of President Hussein's gamble in the light of Weber's comments about legitimation through charisma: "The charismatic leader gains and maintains authority solely by proving his strength in life. If he wants to be a prophet, he must perform miracles; if he wants to be a war lord, he must perform heroic deeds. Above all, however, his divine mission must 'prove' itself in that those who faithfully surrender to him must fare well. If they do not fare well, he is obviously not the master sent by the gods" ("The Sociology of Charismatic Authority," in *From Max Weber: Essays in Sociology*, ed. and trans. Hans H. Gerth and C. Wright Mills [New York: Oxford University Press, 1946], p. 249).

4. As though oil were a small matter for industrial societies.

5. *New York Times*, September 6, 1990, A7.

6. For the full report, see Joel Brinkley, "Divided Loyalties," *New York Times Magazine*, December 16, 1990, sec. 6, beginning p. 36.

7. Bruce Lawrence, "Holy War (Jihad) in Islamic Religion and Nation-State Ideologies," in Kelsay and Johnson, *Just War and Jihad*, pp. 142–143.

8. There are a number of convenient and interesting biographies of Muhammad in English. See, e.g., W. Montgomery Watt, *Muhammad: Prophet and Statesman* (London: Oxford University Press, 1961); and Maxime Rodinson, *Mohammed*, trans. Anne Carter (New York: Pantheon Books, 1971).

9. The verses in the Qur'an are not collected in the order in which they are held to have been revealed. The revealed ordering of verses relies on accounts of the Prophet's life, while the order of the Qur'anic text is a matter of length: longer collections of verses first, shorter collections afterward.

10. Ibn Ishaq, *The Life of Muhammad*, trans. A. Guillaume (New York: Oxford University Press, 1955), pp. 212–213. The Qur'an citation is from 22:40.

11. See n. 5 above.

Chapter Two

1. In Paul Ramsey, *The Just War: Force and Political Responsibility* (Savage, Md.: Littlefield, Adams Quality Paperbacks, 1983), p. 4.

2. In Ibn Ishaq, *Life of Muhammad*, p. 651.

3. Ibid., p. 232.

4. As noted in chapter 1, "classical" indicates the period of Abbasid rule (ca. 750–1258 C.E.), when those patterns of culture considered characteristic of Islamic civilization developed.

5. In particular, by Abdulaziz Sachedina, in his book *Islamic Messianism: The Idea of the Mahdi in Twelver Shiʿism* (Albany, N.Y.: State University of New York Press, 1981).

6. See Abdulaziz Sachedina, "The Development of Jihad in Islamic Revelation and History," in Johnson and Kelsay, *Cross, Crescent, and Sword.*

7. See the collection of Khumayni's speeches and writings in Ruhollah A. Khumayni, *Islam and Revolution: Writings and Declarations of Imam Khomeini,* trans. and annotated by Hamid Algar (Berkeley, Calif.: Mizan Press, 1981).

8. Printed in the *New York Times,* July 23, 1988, A5, in connection with the cease-fire in the war with Iraq. I am grateful to Professor Ann Mayer for this reference.

9. Mahmud Shaltut, *The Koran and Fighting,* in *Jihad in Mediaeval and Modern Islam,* trans. Rudolph Peters (Leiden: E. J. Brill, 1977).

10. Ibid., p. 51.

11. Johannes J. G. Jansen, *The Neglected Duty: The Creed of Sadat's Assassins and the Resurgence of Islamic Militance in the Middle East* (New York: Macmillan Co., 1986).

Chapter Three

1. Max Weber, "The Social Psychology of the World's Religions," in Gerth and Mills, *From Max Weber.*

2. Roland Bainton, *Christian Attitudes Toward War and Peace* (Nashville: Abingdon Press, 1960).

3. For critical discussion of the "Bainton thesis," see Johnson, *Just War Tradition and the Restraint of War;* LeRoy Walters, "The Just War and the Crusade: Antitheses or Analogies?" *The Monist,* 57/4 (October 1973): 584–594; and David Little, " 'Holy War' Appeals and Western Christianity: A Reconsideration of Bainton's Approach," in Kelsay and Johnson, *Just War and Jihad.*

4. Bernard Lewis, "The Roots of Muslim Rage," *Atlantic Monthly*, September 1990, p. 49.

5. For 8:39, the citation here and elsewhere in this chapter follows A. J. Arberry, trans., *The Koran Interpreted* (New York: Macmillan Co., 1964).

6. The language of "divinely sanctioned" or "divinely commanded" should not be taken to imply the necessity of a "divine command theory of ethics" in connection with Islamic thought on war. The relationships between religion and morality in Islam are quite complex. I make some comments on them in the conclusions to this chapter.

7. This version of the *hadith* is taken from the translation of the Hanafi scholar al-Shaybani's *Kitab al-Siyar* by Majid Khadduri, published as *The Islamic Law of Nations* (Baltimore: Johns Hopkins University Press, 1966), sec. 1 of the text. N.B.: *fay*ʾ (untranslated in the citation), like *ghanima*, indicates booty. The distinctions between the categories are disputed. See Khadduri's introduction, pp. 48–49.

8. The term "sovereigns' war" as applied to Iraq's self-understanding is taken from Shahram Chubin and Charles Tripp, *Iran and Iraq at War* (London: I. B. Tauris and Co., 1988). My analysis of the conflict follows these authors closely.

9. Chubin and Tripp, *Iran and Iraq at War*, p. 38 (quoting here as elsewhere from FBIS and BBC/SWB sources).

10. Ibid.

11. Ibid.

12. As noted in chapter 1 of the present volume, Saddam Hussein's appeals to Islam increased as the war with Iran wore on and became central during the Gulf War. Khumayni's characterization of the mixture of Arabism and Islam that Hussein inherited from Gamal Abd al-Nasser relates to a long-standing set of polemics concerning the advisability of mixing the language of ethnicity with that of Islam. For Khumayni, "secularism" implied in particular the lack of a commitment to government according to religious values; he called this "corruption."

13. Chubin and Tripp, *Iran and Iraq at War*, p. 50.

14. This point is somewhat controversial. My understanding is that the Iranians were accused by Iraq of resorting to chemicals but that no evidence could be produced to substantiate the charge.

15. Chubin and Tripp, *Iran and Iraq at War*, p. 55.

16. Ibid.

17. Ibid.

18. Ibid., p. 60.

19. Ibid., p. 59.

20. Ibid., p. 67.

21. Ibid.

22. The one fault line in this argument, so far as I can tell, lies in the Iranian government's reluctance to resolve the war through negotiations. In that case, the conception of war as a defense of religious values apparently justified, for a long while, resistance to any settlement short of the Iraqi government's abdication. Again, the justice of the cause justified great expenditures of human and other resources on the part of Iran. Chubin and Tripp's comment is apposite: "In practice, Iran's sensitivity on the matter of casualties was more pronounced when it came to those of Iraq than when it concerned its own" (*Iran and Iraq at War*, p. 50).

23. Sachedina, in "The Development of Jihad in Islamic Revelation and History," in Johnson and Kelsay, *Cross, Crescent, and Sword*.

Chapter Four

1. Robert Phillips, "Combatancy, Noncombatancy, and Noncombatant Immunity in Just War Tradition," in Johnson and Kelsay, *Cross, Crescent, and Sword*.

2. Ramsey, *The Just War*, pp. 143–144; cf. idem, *War and the Christian Conscience: How Shall Modern War Be Conducted Justly?* (Durham, N.C.: Duke University Press, 1961), ch. 3.

3. John C. Ford, S.J., "The Morality of Obliteration Bombing," as printed in Richard A. Wasserstrom, ed., *War and Morality* (Belmont, Calif.: Wadsworth Publishing Company, 1970), pp. 21f.

4. Johnson, *Just War Tradition and the Restraint of War*, p. 145.

5. Al-Shaybani, as translated by Khadduri, in *The Islamic Law of Nations*, sec. 1. The full text as translated is quoted in chapter 3 of this volume, pp. 46–47 above.

6. Ibid., secs. 28, 29, 30, and 47.

7. See Fred Donner, "The Sources of Islamic Conceptions of War," in Kelsay and Johnson, *Just War and Jihad*.

8. Cf. al-Shaybani, secs. 21–25.

9. See Ibn Rushd (better known in the West as Averroes, d. 1198), Bidayat al-Mujtahid, in Peters, *Jihad in Mediaeval and Modern Islam*, esp. pp. 15–17.

10. Ibid., pp. 11ff.

11. Besides Ibn Rushd, cf. al-Shaybani, secs. 94 and following; also Ibn Taymiyya, *Siyasah al-Shari*a*, trans. as *Public and Private Law in Islam*, by Omar A. Farrukh (Beirut: Khayat's, 1966), esp. pp. 140–143).

12. See al-Shaybani, secs. 28, 30. In the prophetic reports cited in these sections, the rationale for protecting children is that they have not reached puberty, or are minors—i.e., they are not fully responsible to accept or refuse the call to Islam.

13. See Michael Walzer, *Just and Unjust Wars* (New York: Basic Books, 1977), pp. 138–159.

14. Al-Shaybani, secs. 117–123.

15. *Sahih Muslim*, hadith number 4321, trans. Abdul Hamid Siddiqi (Lahore: Sh. Muhammad Ashraf, 1981). See also al-Shaybani, secs. 112–113.

16. Al-Shaybani, secs. 72–81.

17. Ibid., sec. 71.

18. Ibid., secs. 242–257.

19. Ibid., secs. 336ff.

20. Ibid., secs. 88–89. The Qur'an citation is from 59:5.

21. Ibid., sec. 117.

22. Ibid., sec. 119.

23. For further discussion, see John Kelsay, "Religion, Morality, and the Governance of War," *Journal of Religious Ethics*, 18/2 (Fall 1990): 123–139.

24. One should note, however, that just war thinking can qualify the distinction between soldiers and civilians in this way: "Civilians," in the fullest sense, are those whose work or function supports the soldier qua person—that is, provides for the soldier's needs as a human being rather than as a military actor. See James F. Childress's discussion of "Just-War Criteria," in *Moral Responsibility in Conflicts: Essays on Nonviolence, War, and Conscience* (Baton Rouge, La.: Louisiana State University Press, 1982); also see Walzer, *Just and Unjust Wars*, p. 146.

25. A more complete treatment of this topic will be provided in the discussion of irregular war, chapter 5 of this volume.

26. Al-Shaybani, sec. 1372.

27. Ibid., secs. 1373–1374.

28. Ibid., sec. 1394.

29. Ibid., secs. 1401–1404.

30. Ibid., secs. 1417–1420.

31. Ibid., sec. 1444.

32. Ibid., secs. 1379–1380.

33. Ibid., secs. 1381–1386.

34. A convenient source for many of these documents is Yehuda Lukacs, ed., *Documents on the Israeli-Palestinian Conflict, 1967–1983* (Cambridge: Cambridge University Press, 1984). In the light of comments made by those hearing an earlier version of this chapter, I think it important to state that I am treating certain ideas that PLO leaders have articulated as one example of a trend in contemporary Islamic cultural discussion of war. I do not intend my discussion as a comment on current moves by the PLO leadership, or by other Palestinians, in connection with the peace process in the Middle East.

35. In Lukacs, *Documents*, p. 144.

36. Article 22 of the 1968 Palestine National Covenant, in Lukacs, *Documents*, p. 142.

37. During an earlier discussion of the issues addressed in this chapter, Professor Robert Phillips and I exchanged thoughts about the logic of the following statement made by Popular Front for the Liberation of Palestine leader George Habash:

> In the age of the revolution of peoples oppressed by the world im-
> perialist system there can be no geographical or political bound-
> aries or moral limits to the operations of the people's camp. In
> today's world no one is "innocent" and no one is a "neutral" (*Time*
> magazine, April 12, 1970, p. 32).

Phillips argued that it makes little sense for those who hold such views
to object when their own civilians are killed by the military actions of
enemies. (See his essay "Combatancy, Noncombatancy, and Noncombatant Immunity in Just War Tradition" esp. pp. 187–188.) I responded,
and still believe, that the point of such objections is actually that enemy
forces (e.g., those of the United States or the Israelis) commit such acts
in the service of a cause that is by definition unjust. The fact that
women and children are killed simply magnifies the injustice of these
forces.

38. Lukacs, *Documents*, p. 174. Emphasis added.

39. Ibid., p. 145.

40. This point is corroborated by (as yet unpublished) interviews
conducted with Palestinians in 1988–1989 by David Little of the
United States Institute of Peace.

41. Mahmud Shaltut, *The Koran and Fighting*, in Peters, *Jihad in Mediaeval and Modern Islam*.

42. Ibid., p. 27.

43. Ibid., p. 28.

44. Ibid., p. 58.

45. Ibid., pp. 60ff.

46. Ibid., p. 65.

47. Translated as *The Neglected Duty* by Johannes J. G. Jansen. I
shall return to this text, briefly mentioned in an earlier chapter, in the
discussion of irregular war.

48. Sec. 121 of the text as translated by Jansen.

49. Ibid., sec. 122.

50. Bruce Lawrence, "Holy War (Jihad) in Islamic Religion and Nation-State Ideologies," in Kelsay and Johnson, *Just War and Jihad*.

51. Quoted in Chubin and Tripp, *Iran and Iraq at War*, p. 43.

52. Ibid., p. 50.

53. Ibid.

54. Ibid.

55. United Nations Security Council, Document S/16962, "Prisoners of War in Iran and Iraq."

Chapter Five

1. Francis Lieber, "Guerrilla Parties Considered with Reference to the Laws and Usages of War," in Richard Shelly Hartigan, *Lieber's Code and the Law of War* (Chicago: Precedent Publishing, 1983), p. 34. For this and other references to Lieber, I am indebted to the excellent essay by Courtney S. Campbell, "Moral Responsibility and Irregular War," in Johnson and Kelsay, *Cross, Crescent, and Sword* (see quote at p. 106).

2. "Instructions for the Government of Armies of the United States in the Field," (more generally known as *General Orders No. 100*), I.15, in Hartigan, *Lieber's Code*, p. 48. Cited in Campbell, p. 103.

3. Hartigan, *Lieber's Code*, p. 2. Cited in Campbell, p. 104.

4. Ibid., p. 43. Cited in Campbell, p. 106.

5. Johnson, *Just War Tradition and the Restraint of War*, p. 50.

6. See ibid.

7. Lieber, "Guerrilla Parties," in Hartigan, *Lieber's Code*, pp. 33–34, 41. Cited in Campbell, p. 106.

8. Lieber, "Guerrilla Parties," in Hartigan, p. 33.

9. Johnson, *Just War Tradition and the Restraint of War*, p. 50.

10. Lieber, "Guerrilla Parties," in Hartigan, *Lieber's Code*, p. 39.

11. One version of this tradition may be found in *Sahih Muslim: being traditions of the sayings and doings of the Prophet Muhammad as narrated by his companions and compiled under the title al-Jami'us-Sahih*, trans. Abdul Hamid Siddiqi (Lahore: Sh. M. Ashraf, 1976), 4: 1342, report no. 6135. Readers wishing to explore the *fitna* further should consult, among others, Marshall G. S. Hodgson, *The Venture of Islam* (Chicago: University of Chicago Press, 1974), 1:212ff.

12. Al-Shaybani, as translated by Khadduri, in *The Islamic Law of Nations*, sec. 1372.

13. Khaled Abou El Fadl, "Ahkam al-Bughat: Irregular Warfare and the Law of Rebellion in Islam," in Johnson and Kelsay, *Cross, Crescent, and Sword*, p. 153. I owe the Qur'an citation that follows to Abou El Fadl.

14. Taken from James Robson's translation of *Mishkat al-Masabih* (Lahore: Sh. M. Ashraf, 1963–1964), 2:780–782. The *Mishkat* is a traditionally popular compilation developed from the more "canonical" collections of Prophetic sayings (e.g., al-Bukhari's or Abu Muslim's).

15. On the points that follow, I am deeply indebted to the essay by Khaled Abou El Fadl, "Ahkam al-Bughat."

16. Abou El Fadl, "Ahkam al-Bughat," p. 162.

17. Ibid.

18. On the Assassins, see Marshall G. S. Hodgson, *The Order of Assassins* (The Hague: Mouton & Co., 1955).

19. Abou El Fadl, "Ahlsam al-Bughat," p. 167.

20. As in Chubin and Tripp, *Iran and Iraq at War*, p. 38.

21. H. A. R. Gibb, *The Life of Saladin* (Oxford: Clarendon Press, 1973).

22. In this essay, I quote, with some alteration for English idiom, from the translation by Muhammad Maqdsi titled *Charter of the Islamic Resistance Movement (Hamas) of Palestine* (Dallas: Islamic Association for Palestine, 1990). This passage, from Article 15 of the *Charter*, may be found at p. 22 of Maqdsi's translation. Please note: the views expressed within the Hamas Charter do not represent those of the Islamic Association for Palestine (IAP). The translation is used with the permission of IAP.

23. Ibid. Emphasis in original.

24. Ibid., p. 28 (art. 22). The reference to the destruction of the Caliphate points to the abolition of that institution by the Turks in 1924. Readers will note that, in this and other passages, the Hamas Charter mingles specifically Islamic notions with ideas characteristic of classic European anti-Semitism. In article 32 (p. 38 of the Maqdsi translation), for example, the *Charter* cites the "Protocols of the Elders of Zion" as evidence of a Jewish conspiracy to dominate the world. For a discussion of this text, which has proven so destructive in Europe and North America, see Norman Cohn, *Warrant for Genocide: The Myth of the Jewish World-Conspiracy and the Protocols of the Elders of Zion* (New

York: Harper & Row, 1967). For a more general discussion of the role of European (including National Socialist) anti-Semitic ideas and writings in contemporary Arab and Islamic thought, see (among others) Bernard Lewis, *Semites and Anti-Semites: An Inquiry Into Conflict and Prejudice* (New York: W. W. Norton, 1986).

25. Ibid., p. 29 (art. 22).

26. Ibid., p. 38 (art. 32).

27. Ibid., pp. 17–18 (arts. 11, 12). Emphasis in original.

28. Ibid., p. 21 (art. 15). My emphasis.

29. Ibid., p. 22 (art. 15). These are selections from the sayings of the Prophet. I have inserted the word *undertakes* according to the sense of the original.

30. Ibid., p. 37 (art. 31). My insertions.

31. On Arafat, see chapter 4.

32. Hamas *Charter*, p. 13 (art. 6).

33. Muhammad Hussein Fadlallah, "To Avoid a World War of Terror," *Washington Post*, April 6, 1986, C5.

34. Translated by Johannes J. G. Jansen, *The Neglected Duty* first became widely known when the Shaykh al-Azhar published a refutation of it, parts of which were excerpted in Egyptian newspapers in December 1981. The Shaykh's intent was to refute the reasoning of the group that had assassinated Sadat in October of that year. Subsequently, other newspapers printed versions of the militants' text, and a number of Islamic authorities joined the Shaykh al-Azhar in criticizing its arguments. The history of the text, speculation about its author(s), and discussion of the various responses are all included in Jansen's work. On authorship, in particular, the text has the appearance of a "school" or "movement" text that builds on conversations in which several people have participated. For convenience, however, I refer in the discussion that follows to "the author."

35. Jansen, *The Neglected Duty*, p. 160.

36. Ibid., pp. 192–193.

37. Ibid., pp. 179–181.

38. Ibid., 191–192, 165–166, 166–167, 167–168, and 169–172, respectively.

39. Ibid., p. 191.

40. Ibid.

41. Ibid., pp. 191–192.

42. Ibid., p. 192.

43. Ibid., pp. 166–167.

44. Ibid., p. 169.

45. Ibid., pp. 169–170.

46. Ibid., p. 198.

47. Ibid., p. 211.

48. Ibid., pp. 211ff.

49. Ibid., p. 212.

50. Ibid., p. 210.

51. Ibid., pp. 215–216.

52. Ibid., pp. 217–218.

53. Ibid., pp. 208–209.

54. Summarized by Jansen, *The Neglected Duty*, pp. 35–62.

55. Jansen, *The Neglected Duty*, p. 199.

56. Ibid.

57. Ibid., p. 200.

58. Selections published as "To Avoid a World War of Terror," in the *Washington Post*, April 6, 1986, C5.

59. Ibid.

60. Ibid.

61. Ibid. In November of 1992, I presented some of the material from this chapter as part of the Ethics section at the American Academy of Religion meeting in San Francisco. One of those attending asked about the relevance of my discussion to the conflict between Serbs, Croats, and Muslims in Bosnia, which has, especially for the Muslims, attained critical proportions since this chapter was sent to the publisher in June, 1992. Given Shaykh Fadlallah's just-quoted warning about the connections between injustice and irregular war, I

wish to add the following comments. From a Western, just-war point of view, the Bosnian Serbs who, in particular, are charged with carrying out a program of "ethnic cleansing" against Bosnian Muslims may be "irregulars." From the point of view of many Muslims, the more significant fact about these Serbs (and, to a lesser extent, Croatians) is their connection with the struggle to establish a "greater Serbia" (or Croatia). In the case of Serbs, of course, this notion has been articulated by Slobodan Milosevic and other leaders. According to this point of view, the Serbian forces in Bosnia are "crusaders," armies in the service of an established regime that conspires to eliminate the influence of Islam in a particular region. Correlatively, the failure of the international community to respond with sufficient strength to alleviate the suffering of Bosnia's Muslims is taken as confirmation that the position articulated by groups like Hamas or Islamic Jihad is correct: the West is implacably hostile to Islam, even in the "pro-Western" form presented by Bosnian Muslims, and intends to limit its influence as much as possible. At the same time, so-called Muslim leaders do not come to Bosnia's aid because they are really the servants of the West. The international discussion of intervention in Bosnia ought to take account of the long-term political consequences suggested by the ways that the current tragedy serves to confirm the analysis of the world offered in such texts as *The Neglected Duty* and the *Charter* of Hamas.

Chapter Six

1. Text of the speech in the *New York Times*, October 2, 1990, A6.

2. Ibid.

3. "Bush Stands Firm on Military Policy in Iraqi Civil War," *New York Times*, April 14, 1991, A1.

4. Front page of the September 1–15, 1990, issue.

5. Muhammad Yusuf, "Who Speaks for the Muslims of Palestine?" *Crescent International*, December 16–31, 1991, p. 3.

6. As per Paul Fussell, *The Rhetorical World of Augustan Humanism: Ethics and Imagery from Swift to Burke* (Oxford: Clarendon Press, 1965), p. 4.

7. *New York Times*, February 16, 1991, A5.

8. See Richard Rubenstein, *After Auschwitz*, 2nd ed. (Baltimore: Johns Hopkins University Press, 1992), and other works.

9. *New York Times*, Dec. 15, 1990, A17.

10. The proceedings of the forum are summarized in David R. Smock, *Religious Perspectives on War: Christian, Muslim, and Jewish Attitudes Toward Force After the Gulf War* (Washington, D.C.: United States Institute of Peace Press, 1992).

11. For details, see ibid., pp. 15–22.

12. For details, see ibid., pp. 23f.

Select Bibliography

A number of useful sources are mentioned in the notes to the various chapters of this book. This brief list is intended as a guide for further reading and focuses on works readily available to English-speaking readers.

Ajami, Fouad. *The Arab Predicament: Arab Political Thought and Practice Since 1967.* New York: Cambridge University Press, 1981.

An important interpretation of trends in Arab political thought in the post-1967 period. *The Vanished Imam: Musa al Sadr and the Shia of Lebanon* (Ithaca, N.Y.: Cornell University Press, 1986) by the same author provides an interesting account of the development of the Shiite community and its role in Lebanese politics during the 1970s and 1980s.

Bainton, Roland. *Christian Attitudes Toward War and Peace: A Historical Survey and Critical Re-evaluation.* Nashville: Abingdon Press, 1960.

A basic and important survey of diverse approaches to war in the Christian tradition: pacifism, just war, and holy war/crusade.

Bill, James A. *The Eagle and the Lion: The Tragedy of American-Iranian Relations.* New Haven, Conn.: Yale University Press, 1988.

A thorough study of the breakdown in relations that contributed to U.S.-Iranian enmity following the Islamic Revolution of 1978–1979.

Childress, James F. *Moral Responsibility in Conflicts: Essays on Nonviolence, War, and Conscience.* Baton Rouge, La.: Louisiana State University Press, 1982.

An influential study by a leading scholar of religious ethics, this book includes Childress's essays on the bases and interrelationship of the just war criteria and on Francis Lieber's treatment of the laws of war.

Hodgson, Marshall G. S. *The Venture of Islam: Conscience and History in a World Civilization.* 3 vols. Chicago: University of Chicago Press, 1974.

Remains the best English-language survey of the history of Islamic religion and culture.

Johnson, James Turner. *Just War Tradition and the Restraint of War: A Moral and Historical Inquiry.* Princeton, N. J.: Princeton University Press, 1981.

A seminal study by a distinguished historian of just war tradition. The work should be supplemented by the same author's *Ideology, Reason, and the Limitation of War: Religious and Secular Concepts, 1200–1740.* (Princeton, N.J.: Princeton University Press, 1975), *Can Modern War Be Just?* (New Haven, Conn.: Yale University Press, 1984), and *The Quest for Peace: Three Moral Traditions in Western Cultural History* (Princeton, N.J.: Princeton University Press, 1987).

Johnson, James Turner, and John Kelsay, eds. *Cross, Crescent, and Sword: The Justification and Limitation of War in Western and Islamic Tradition.* Contributions to the Study of Religion, vol. 27. Westport, Conn.: Greenwood Press, 1990.

Together with a companion volume titled *Just War and Jihad: Historical and Theoretical Perspectives on War and Peace in Western and Islamic Traditions* (Westport, Conn.: Greenwood Press, 1991), presents a collection of papers by leading scholars in ethics and Islamic studies comparing Western and Islamic perspectives on the interrelationship between religion, society, and war.

Lewis, Bernard. *The Political Language of Islam.* Chicago: University of Chicago Press, 1988.

An analysis of political dimensions of the Islamic tradition by the best known of contemporary Western historians of Islam.

Little, David, John Kelsay, and Abdulaziz Sachedina. *Human Rights and the Conflict of Cultures*. Columbia, S.C.: University of South Carolina Press, 1988.

Focuses on the status of freedom of conscience and religious liberty in Western and Islamic traditions.

Miller, Richard B. *Interpretations of Conflict: Ethics, Pacifism, and the Just-War Tradition*. Chicago: University of Chicago Press, 1991.

A fine discussion of the relationship between pacifism and just war thinking in Western religious and moral traditions.

Peters, R. *Jihad in Mediaeval and Modern Islam*. Leiden, Netherlands: E. J. Brill, 1977.

Contains translations of discussions of the Islamic approach to war by Averroes, the great medieval scholar, and by the late Shaykh al-Azhar, Mahmud Shaltut.

Piscatori, James, ed. *Islamic Fundamentalisms and the Gulf Crisis*. Chicago: The Fundamentalism Project/American Academy of Arts and Sciences, 1991.

Essays by a variety of writers on the responses of militant groups to the Gulf Crisis.

Ramsey, Paul. *War and the Christian Conscience: How Shall Modern War Be Conducted Justly?* Durham, N.C.: Duke University Press, 1961.

This work represents Ramsey's basic interpretation of the just war tradition as the outcome of Christian efforts to live according to the love command. Together with his *The Just War: Force and Political Responsibility* (New York: Charles Scribner's Sons, 1968; reprint, Savage, Md.: Littlefield, Adams Quality Paperbacks, 1983) and *Speak Up for Just War or Pacifism* (University Park, Pa.: Pennsylvania State University Press, 1988), the book presents a thorough and powerful argument concerning the relationship of the just war tradition to modern war.

Sachedina, Abdulaziz A. *The Just Ruler in Shiʿite Islam: The Comprehensive Authority of the Jurist in Imamite Jurisprudence.* New York: Oxford University Press, 1988.

A scholarly study of the Shiite tradition on political authority, the volume complements Sachedina's previous work on the historical and doctrinal development of Twelver or Imami Shiʿism: *Islamic Messianism: The Idea of Mahdi in Twelver Shiʿism* (Albany, N.Y.: State University of New York Press, 1981).

Schacht, Joseph. "Islamic Religious Law." *The Legacy of Islam,* 2nd ed., ed. Joseph Schacht with C. E. Bosworth. London: Oxford University Press, 1974.

An important and concise summary of the history and theory of Islamic jurisprudence.

al-Shaybani, Muhammad ibn al-Hasan. *The Islamic Law of Nations.* Ed. and trans. Majid Khadduri. Baltimore: Johns Hopkins University Press, 1966.

A translation of the treatise of a late eighth/early ninth century Islamic scholar on the rules governing interactions between the territory of Islam and the territory of war. Khadduri's introduction is very helpful. *War and Peace in the Law of Islam* (New York: AMS Press, 1979), by Khadduri, was first published in 1953. It remains the most complete survey of Islamic teaching on the rules of war available to readers of English.

Sifry, Micah L., and Christopher Cerf, eds. *The Gulf War Reader: History, Documents, Opinions.* New York: Times Books/Random House, 1991.

A useful collection of documents and articles exploring various dimensions of the crisis and war that followed Iraq's invasion of Kuwait.

United States Conference of Catholic Bishops. *The Challenge of Peace.* Washington, D.C.: National Conference of Catholic Bishops, 1983.

This pastoral letter, which attracted a great deal of public attention due to its careful treatment of the issues surrounding nuclear deterrence, should be supplemented by a follow-up document, *Building Peace* (Washington, D.C.: National Conference of Catholic Bishops, 1988).

Walters, LeRoy. "The Just War and the Crusade: Antitheses or Analogies?" *The Monist* 57, no. 4 (October 1973): 584–594.

Contains Walters's important criticisms of Roland Bainton's discussion of holy war.

Walzer, Michael. *Just and Unjust Wars: A Moral Argument with Historical Illustrations.* New York: Basic Books, 1977.

Perhaps the leading secular interpretation of the just war tradition, this book illustrates the just war criteria through discussion of historical examples.

Index

Printed in the United States
1796